MASTER IN SAIL

MASTER IN SAIL

Captain William Murchison

NAVIGATOR BOOKS

Published by Navigator Books
Ringwood, Hampshire

ISBN 0 902830 58 9

Typeset by Moorhouse Typesetters
Printed by The Cromwell Press, Melksham, Wiltshire

CHAPTER ONE

I often told tales about my native parish and about the sea to my children; and now that they have grown up, they keep at me to write all these old stories down. I have neither the competence nor the education to write a story, as I had very little schooling. Therefore my English is very bad and my grammar worse. I don't even feel that my stories are worth putting down on paper.

I was born in Toscaig in the Parish of Applecross, Ross-shire on February 4th, 1884. Applecross is a peninsula between Loch Torridon on the North and Loch Carron on the South. The road from the end of Loch Kishorn - an arm of Loch Carron - goes up in many zig-zags till it reaches to the top of Bealach-Nam-Bo, 2,100 feet high, and descends to Applecross Bay on the other side, which is less tortuous than that going up. Someone said that Applecross was like Heaven; difficult to get there, but one wouldn't want to leave when one settled there.

Toscaig is a small village connected with Applecross village by a gravel road, which was constructed by the Proprietor, MacKenzie, about 1846 to give employment to the people. The potato crop had been a failure and the people had very little to eat. Toscaig village had about 24 crofts when I was a boy. All the men were seafaring, either fishing or going away south to join the mercantile marine. It is therefore not surprising that I took to the sea. I even remember a man taking his two year old son into a boat and wetting his lips and tongue with sea water. This was a sure cure for sea sickness.

Most of my ancestors, in both my mother's and father's families, were either fishermen or seamen. On my father's side my great grandmother's brother, Donald Red Campbell, was very well known on the west coast. He was the owner of a small schooner during the Napoleonic Wars and traded regularly between the South and the North-West Highlands. When he got ashore and free from responsibility he was quite ready to go to the local pub and have a few drinks. When he called at Loch Carron - his native village - and when he had had a few drams, the local boys would shout at him and call him the finest sailor on the West Coast. He invariably threw pennies to them and so there was no one more welcome in his own village.

His nephew, my grandfather's brother, when very young, was gathering seaweed one day and he slipped and broke his leg and was lame all his life. His father said that he would not be able to do anything except tailoring or shoemaking. So he was apprenticed to a shoemaker, in fact his own sister's husband. He, however, ran away with his jovial uncle to sea and in due course became a merchant and small shipowner with his own smacks. He was a very shrewd man and was also supposed to be very hard in all his dealings. Stories about him are quoted to this day. Once, on hearing that a man who owed him 5/- was seriously ill, he sent a special messenger to collect it before he died. The messenger had to walk 40 miles. It was never divulged how much of the 5/- he got. He was known as the Duie.

* * *

I have been going ahead too fast. My great-grandfather, John Murchison, was born about 1750 in Achnashellach, a lovely glen about 7 miles from the head of Loch Carron. He married there a Mary Campbell, about 1790 or earlier. Presumably he had a croft there. The farms were small in those days, for I believe there were 42 families in the glen for some years, probably more than 50 years after the 1745 rebellion. The glen was famous for its fat cattle and sheep and it seems very likely the small farmers of the glen were fairly well off, especially during the Napoleonic Wars when Highland cattle fetched good prices. They were driven on the foot to Falkirk and then sent on to Norfolk for wintering. The general opinion of those days was that without the Highland cattle the British Navy could not exist, let alone fight.

Shortly after the Wars came to an end the people were cleared out of Achnashellach. John's eldest son was the Duie. By the time of the Clearances the second eldest son of the family, Finlay, was married in Loch Carron and, presumably, John Murchison and his wife lived with the second eldest son as was the custom in those days. In any case they went to Applecross with him about 1833 and died there at a ripe old age.

This son and his family of 12 went to the U.S.A. about 1851. There was such a commotion the morning they were leaving and boarding the ship, which was anchored off Applecross, that the baby was left in the cradle in the house. The mother thought that one of the daughters had the baby and the daughters understood the mother had him. One of the family had to row ashore to get the baby. He was fast asleep in the kitchen.

My grandfather, who was the youngest son of John Murchison, was by now married to an Applecross woman, Jessie MacLean. By 1850 they had a family of 7, and my grandfather was of the opinion that they should follow his brother to the U.S.A. He had settled in Illinois. My grandmother would not hear of it. She was left her father's croft in Uags, Applecross. Her father was well known and was an elder of the kirk in Applecross. When the disruption of the churches occurred in 1843, he was so much against the old Kirk and for the newly formed Free Church that he stood at the crossroads, threatening everyone that he would knock anyone down, who would dare enter the old Kirk. Every Sunday, till he was a very old man, he walked from Uags to the Church, which was 10 miles away. He went barefooted across the moor about 4 miles. He sat down for a rest and put on his shoes and stockings when he got to the gravel. Finally, my grandfather and grandmother settled in Toscaig, Applecross, and that is how I came to be born in that village and brought up there.

When my grandfather left Uags (the South Point of Applecross peninsula) for Toscaig, six of his eight children, John, Finlay (my father), Donald, Mary, Kenneth, Ann, Elizabeth and William, were already born. My father and his eldest brother, John, were working by that time. My father actually started work before he was 11 years old. He went as cook of a smack, leaving home in May of 1848, barefooted, and arrived back home in November, still barefooted. His pay for the whole period was £2.10/- and his keep, or "all found" as they say today. He brought the whole of his wages home to his mother intact.

Later on that Winter he and his brother got an open boat and went fishing to Loch Ainort in Skye. The weather was very bad and their only shelter, when they were at anchor, was the sail. They were not able to take their clothes off for over a week; so when they arrived home my father's feet were so swollen that he was put in front of the fire to thaw and his sea boots had to be cut to get them off his feet.

The five sons naturally took to the sea, and as time went on they got their own fishing boat, and later on they bought schooners in which they traded on the Coast of the Continent, as far north as Iceland and as far south as the North Coast of Africa. One of the schooners was built especially for them in Perth and carried 200 tons of cargo. They prospered to a certain extent but never made much money. I fear that one of the reasons was that they were sailors first and business came second. Furthermore, the three eldest brothers had no education whatsoever.

Life was hard in those days on the north-west coast, but, as the families were not expected to go to school, they helped with the croft, and very often went down to the rocks on the sea, and caught as many fish as would do the whole family's supper in a matter of about an hour. Presumably then, they were never hungry, although poor.

I heard one story quoted about a village called Aird on Loch Carron. The housewife would shout to the boys in bed, 'Get up and go out and fetch your breakfast.' They would run to the shore, launch a boat and within half an hour would be back in the house with more than enough fish for the household for breakfast. Large families in those days were in many respects a great asset. My father said to someone in those days that a few daughters in a household were a far greater asset than a schooner.

* * *

I started to write this story about three years ago while in residence in Edinburgh with my son and daughter, who had bought a house there. When I got home to Loch Carron I found myself so busy with all sorts of things that I found no time to get down to my story. Here I am in a different setting altogether. My wife and I are aboard the S.S. "Southern Cross" in the year 1958, bound for New Zealand. So I have ample time to resume my narrative, although it amazes me how time is wasted by everyone, just mere chattering, walking and games for the young. The ship carries 1,160 passengers.

* * *

Although my father thought daughters a great asset in the household, sons, if they were wise, were a greater asset. Young women in his day went out to service for £6 for six months and, of course, their keep. When my grandfather settled on a croft in Toscaig about 1850 with his family of four boys and three girls (a son was born in Toscaig in 1855), the oldest of the family were working mostly in fishing boats, and occasionally going south in the winter months to work on Railways and Road Building. Before very long, however, that was before 1860, they had purchased a large fishing boat, *"Commodore"*, which was big enough to take them fishing to the East Coast of Scotland, through the Caledonian Canal. An old man in the village who, when a boy of 16, went with them fishing in the East Coast of Scotland, told me that on the way back, after getting through the canal, they set sail for home after daylight in June. They sailed the whole day down Loch Linnhe and through the Sound of Mull and anchored in Toscaig before the sun set: very good fast sailing for a boat of the type then in use with their square sterns. I am not sure what year they gave up fishing, but it would be getting on to the 1870s.

* * *

Here I digress. (I am writing on 27th December 1958). I was lazy on Christmas day and Boxing Day, so lolled about in a beautiful calm day in the Doldrums. Actually, we passed the line on the morning of the 26th. I stood a bottle of champagne to the people at our table on Christmas Day - two New Zealand ladies from Auckland and a man and his daughter from Bristol: quite a nice quiet Christmas. I don't enjoy drink really and have been a teetotaller all my life, at least till very lately.

Anyway, I was wondering as I had nothing to do aboard, how many Christmases I had at home since I left early in 1900. The first three I had at home. In 1903 I was in the Mediterranean; 1904 in Rangoon; 1905 off Tristan Da Cunha; 1906 in Melbourne; 1907 in Honolulu; 1908 in Glasgow; 1909 on the way to Sydney from Calcutta;

1910 bound from Barry for Rio de Janeiro 1911 on the way from U.S.A. to Japan; 1912 on the way to China from U.S.A.; 1913 on the way from Antwerp to Rio de Janeiro; 1914 Glasgow; 1915 Calcutta to Sydney; 1916 hove to in a gale off Cape Finisterre; 1917 East Africa; 1918 South Africa (Durban); 1919 a day out from Delagoa Bay coming from Calcutta; 1920 Basrah, Iraq; from then to 1926 had Christmas in Basrah; 1927 in Loch Carron; from 1928 till 1932 in Basrah; from 1933 till 1938 in Baghdad; 1939 in Basrah; 1940 on way by flying boat from Basrah to Durban; 1941, 42, 43, in Basrah; 1944 in Loch Carron; 1945 in Baghdad; 1946 in Baghdad; 1947 and 48 in Baghdad; 1949 in Edinburgh; 1950 and 51 in Baghdad; 1952 in Baghdad; 1953 in Loch Carron; 1954 on the way to New Zealand on S.S. "Scottish Star"; 1955 in Loch Carron; 1956 and 57 Loch Carron; 1958 on S.S. "Southern Cross" in Pacific on the way to New Zealand.

* * *

Now to continue about my grandfather's family. Earlier than 1870 his four eldest sons bought a schooner. They were John, Finlay, Donald and Kenneth. The schooner was named the *"Jessie"* after their mother. Later on they bought another schooner, which was named the *"Surprise"*. John was master, as a rule, in the *"Surprise"*, but as he had no education and could not read or write he had to employ a sailing master, that is, a man who was acquainted with the Foreign Trade and had experience of foreign sailing. Anywhere on the continent between the Elbe and Brest was considered as coasting trade, so a sailing master was not necessary, but beyond these limits, either north or south, it was called foreign trade and all ships going beyond the aforesaid limits had, on entering and sailing from a port in the U.K., to submit all the documents of ship and cargo to the Custom House. On one occasion when the *"Surprise"* was in the Baltic with John in command, the sailing master aboard got on drunk, so John had to leave him behind and he took the *"Surprise"* from the Kattegat to the Pentland Firth himself. He told the seamen on the look out to look for the Skerries Lighthouse at a certain time and, sure enough, the lighthouse was picked up at the time he said. The men aboard were full of admiration for a man who could not read or write to make such a good landfall in such misty weather. Looking back on this incident I think myself he must have been able to set a course on the chart.

At around the year 1875-76 Kenneth was in charge of the schooner *"Jessie"* and he lost her on the Goodwin Sands, while on a voyage with potatoes from a Baltic Port to Cork or maybe Waterford. It was thick, nasty weather. They got out of the wreck on a raft and were picked up by the Deal Lifeboat. I think most of the crew were from Applecross. In fact, the crews of the schooners were nearly always Applecross men and boys. I think Kenneth was one of the, if not the, most intelligent member of my grandfather's family. At least he certainly was an extremely able seaman. I often heard stories about his capabilities in sailing boats. On one occasion, coming in an open boat from Lochalsh to Applecross with a large crowd of women aboard, who had been at a communion in Ardelve, he was asked to take the helm, as the wind and sea were increasing, for the women were all certain that he was the only man who could deliver them safely at Toscaig. Women, of course, get too easily frightened in a sailing boat, especially when she heels over to a good strong wind. In any case, some of the women who were in the boat that day often told me, when I was a boy, that they were saved by the Grace of God and steersmanship of Kenneth Murchison.

On another occasion I was sincerely told by the Blacksmith, William Gordon in Kishorn, that when he was a boy, probably 15 or 16 years, he was one of the crew of the fishing boat *"Commodore"* with Kenneth as skipper, and in the Minch they were caught in a gale. His own words - that is, William Gordon's - were that they were saved by the capable helmsman, Kenneth Murchison.

After the schooner *"Jessie"* was lost, the brothers were talking of buying another schooner, but meantime John was in Dundee in the *"Surprise"* and after a few drinks with Allison, the sail-maker there, John ordered a schooner to be built in Perth for them. The brothers were rather annoyed, especially Kenneth. The eldest brother, John, was more convivial than the others and it was often said of him that he was too fond of the bottle, whereas Kenneth was a teetotaller. However, thc schooner was built and Kenneth was skipper of her. He was only two years in school, but had a remarkable grasp of the English language and did his own chartering and ship's business.

* * *

New Year's Day, 1959, and we passed an Atoll in the Tahiti Group of Islands.

* * *

My father was mate of the new schooner. She was called the *"Alpha"* and local people in the Parish of Applecross said it was not lucky to take a name from the Bible for a ship. Anyway, Kenneth had charge of her for a few years, and while on a voyage from the Tyne to Sligo with coal, he was carried by a huge wave from the fore-rigging to the lee bulwark and was badly hurt. Whether that was the cause of his death in 1879 I don't know, but consumption I believe, set in. Probably his lung was hurt and he never paid attention to it. Donald also died shortly before him. These two deaths, so near to each other, were a terrible blow to the family.

The youngest brother, William, took over the command of the *"Alpha"*. He was born about 1855 and was six years younger than the last child, Elizabeth, my grandmother had had. Some people told me that my grandmother was 53 when William was born, but my Aunt Mary questioned this and thought she was between 51 and 52. Anyway, by the time William grew up to eight or nine years, education had come to the Highlands. They were called Church Schools and very often carried through by ladies from Edinburgh. Although compulsory education did not reach the Highlands till after 1874, most of the young men, if they were interested, got educated. For instance, the school in Applecross was at Milton and boys from Toscaig had to walk five miles there and five miles back for any education they could get. I know that Uncle William attended this school, and so did my uncle Norman, my mother's brother.

Uncle William went to sea in the schooners when he was 15 years old and so he was an experienced seaman before his brother Kenneth died, and I believe he had his master's certificate about then. I am not certain, but I think it was in the 60s that it became compulsory for all masters of ships to have certificates issued by the Board of Trade. Father never got above mate, as he had no education, and

Uncle John was always in great difficulty in finding suitable sailing masters for the *"Surprise"*. In fact in the 80s, when he was not well, he had to rely on them far too much and eventually had to sell the schooner some time before he died. Uncle William and father, however, managed to keep the *"Alpha"* going, but one year in the 80s they were nearly ruined through low freights. However, by borrowing £500 they survived. Father borrowed from my mother's sister's husband, a gamekeeper in Jura, and his name was John Murchison. They had no family. He got £250 from him, and Uncle William borrowed £250 from his brother-in-law, a merchant in Applecross. His name was Duncan Murchison - neither of them relations of ours. The *"Alpha"* was in Peterhead at the time. Freights suddenly jumped up and they got a charter for the Baltic to fill up with barrels of herring and got another very good charter back to England, with the result they paid off all the money they had borrowed.

* * *

Saturday, 3rd January 1959. We left Tahiti Island this morning. It is a most fascinating place unspoilt by civilisation.

* * *

To continue with my story, my grandfather died in 1882. Before he died the old house in Upper Toscaig was given to Aunt Mary and her husband and their family. They resided in Lonbain, North Applecross after Aunt Mary got married in the late 60s. Aunt Elizabeth got married to the merchant Duncan Murchison in 1881. So now there was only Aunt Ann, who never married and who lived with grandmother.

Father and Uncle William were always at sea, but father had to come home every Spring to help the women with the work of the croft - very hard work in those days. The ground for planting the potatoes and corn was turned over by a cas-chrom. All the manure was carried in creels, even to the remotest part of the croft. Seaweed had, very often, to be taken over from Crowlin Island in boats. Enormous quantities of this stuff were taken ashore and all had to be carried in creels to the land. Grandfather built a house in Lower Toscaig. At least he engaged masons and joiners to do the job. It was a smallish house - 4 rooms and 2 closets altogether, and the schooner *"Alpha"* brought the slates for the roof from Wales. It was a big improvement on the old black house and was the first white house to be built at the south end of Applecross.

Woman with creel

The years went on, I don't think the schooner was making a great deal of money for the owners, but sufficient to keep them all in fairly good circumstances. Looking back on this period I think they neglected the financial side of the business. The money earned was deposited in the Bank and Uncle William said to me that he was sure some of their money was lost when a certain Bank Manager did the Bank down through gambling. It is just possible, as they were always at sea, and they trusted the Bank implicitly, as they were really good seamen first and finance was of little importance to them so it got second place.

CHAPTER TWO

In 1883 father got married to Kate MacLennan, his next door neighbour while they lived in Upper Toscaig. Father took over her croft, as her father had died a couple of years before, and her mother shortly afterwards. She had an uncle staying with them before she married, so he helped mother to work the croft when father was at sea. Uncle William got married to a Kyleakin woman, Swanson, in 1885, so I think they made their home in Kyleakin for a while.

* * *

I am now in New Zealand and my wife and I are staying with the Campbells at Tauranga, Bay of Plenty. Mrs. Campbell is Proby's aunt, and she is full of old stories.

* * *

But to get back to my own story. After father got married he took his wife to the new house. His mother and his sister Ann, who did not marry, lived at one end of the house and father and mother lived in the other end.

My mother's people came from Balgy, Loch Torridon. They lived there on a croft for generations. Today the place appears to me as very rocky and poor land. I was told, however, by old people, mostly MacLennans (one of them I visited in 1908, age 97, in Shieldaig, a relation of ours) that Balgy was one of the finest lands in the Highlands for good milking cows; in some years the milk would be so plentiful that the women had to use their washing tubs for making cheese. Disaster came to the whole community. They were forced out of their village and the whole place was put under sheep. My great-great-grandfather was a very old man at that time and died shortly afterwards. His wife was about 70. Her son came home from the Continental Wars (I believe Waterloo) to find that his wife, Barbara, had died in childbirth some time before his arrival, and the orders were, that the old people, himself, and the baby, were to get out of their home. As I said, his father had died, but he took his mother with him to Canada, married again before he sailed and I often heard that when he was an old man he could climb a little hill at the back of his house and count eight chimney's smoke, rising from his eight children's own houses and farms. This was my great-grandfather's brother. I also heard stories that two of his brothers, both bachelors, went to California and eventually were gold digging. They got to be very rich. One story that got back to Applecross, from a man who called on them when they were very old, was that they were so rich that they both sat on golden chairs. I imagine, however, that the gold was really gilt. Anyway, their nephew, Roderick MacLennan, received a letter from the U.S.A. (he was my grandfather); before the Post Office would deliver it, my grandfather would have to pay 5/- for the letter; but nobody in those days in the village could read, so everyone said it was a trick and that his rent was to be put up. Eventually, to get rid of this obnoxious document they all thought that the safest thing to do with it was to burn it, which was duly done. Someone told me, years afterwards, that the letter was from the uncles in California, and that they were meaning to leave their money to him and his descendants, but, as they did not hear from my grandfather, they never made a will and the money was taken by the Government.

When the folk in Balgy were chased out of their homes, some went to Canada and some to the U.S.A. There was no emigration to the U.S.A. from the beginning of the War of Independence till after the Battle of Waterloo, when peace reigned (more or less) in Europe. My great-grandfather, Murdo MacLennan, with his family, went to Raasay to a village called Torran, and then to a village in Scalpay (near Skye) called Corran. My great-grandfather meantime died. It was a sad business in those days, hounding people off the land which had been in their possession, perhaps for hundreds of years.

I was told a story by the old man of 97 in Shieldaig, and also by my mother, that the last Sunday night the MacLennans of Balgy attended Church in Shieldaig, the minister (I don't know his name) preached a powerful sermon, indicting those who were responsible for putting the people out of their homes and off the land. There was not a dry eye in the congregation when they left the church. Today in 1959, Balgy has only one gamekeeper's house and the mansion, which was built over 100 years ago for the owner of the deer forest, is becoming an encumbrance to its possessors and will soon have to close - I expect owing to heavy taxation. The old minister, who preached that famous sermon, predicted that that would soon happen in due course, mainly because of the injustice done to the people.

My grandfather, Roderick MacLennan, married while in Corran, Scalpay, a girl named Helen MacLeod. I really know nothing about this woman, except that an old woman told me that she was kind and amiable, and not very tall - average height or just below it. Another old woman, a MacLennan in Shieldaig, was bragging to me one day and said that I should be proud of her, as she was descended from the MacLeods of Raasay.

I heard a story about one of the MacLeods of Raasay from Mrs. Campbell with whom we are now staying (February 1959). She is my wife's aunt. The story is that one day the young Laird of Raasay was out hunting and met a young maiden herding cattle and sheep. He spoke to her, and in due course noticed that she was the finest looking and most intelligent woman he had ever met, and he fell in love with her. He decided, there and then, to send her to Edinburgh to be educated, though this was much against his family's wishes. She got on very well and the next or following year, when the Laird came to Edinburgh, she was so disappointed that he did not call on her first, that she composed the famous Gaelic song, "Thainig an Gille Dubh Raoir do'n Bhaile So". Later on, of course he did call and, in due course, they were married and the Laird took her home to Raasay. His father and family were still incensed at the marriage and when she arrived at the house the father said to her, 'Why did you, Dark Maiden, marry my son?'

'Because, my Lord of Raasay,' she said, 'I had not a better offer.'

From that day onwards they were fast friends.

On or about the year 1864 my grandfather, my mother's father, got a croft in Toscaig, Applecross and he died there in 1882. His son Murdo died at an early age and his daughter, Peggy, aged 24, died of pneumonia. His daughter, Jessie, married John Murchison, Kinlochewe, afterwards gamekeeper in Jura and then sheep farming in Coulin. My grandfather's son Norman went to Sydney, Australia, aged 17.

* * *

April 21st 1959. I again digress. Since we arrived in New Zealand on the 12th January 1959 we have toured the South Island. We were always doing something or other when in residence with Aunt Betta and her husband at Tauranga and had little time to write. We left Auckland on the 2nd April for Sydney where I met relations; Finlay Murchison, Kishorn and my cousins, Jessie and Norman MacLennan. Jessie and Norman were children of my mother's brother, Norman. Jessie is a widow for some six years and Norman, who lost his wife recently, had no family. Jessie, who is now a Mrs. Paisley, had three daughters, one married in America, one still in Australia, now a barrister, and one a doctor in Newfoundland. Norman, my mother's brother mentioned above, married a girl form Glasgow in 1890, age 18. She is still alive, aged 90. I met her before, when voyaging to Australia, but was more interested than ever, this time, as I was able to get a few stories from her.

* * *

Now to get back to my Mother and Father. They were married in the year 1883 in the month of March, (if I remember correctly), and I was born on the 4th February 1884. The schooner *"Alpha"* happened to call on the day of my birth, or rather the night before, at Applecross, and as the weather was good she anchored off Holy Island, Camusterrach, the wind being off the land, S.E. and the anchorage was safe. Father went home, of course, but Uncle and a boy, MacNair, from Aird-dhubh stayed on board. Like a bolt out of the blue, the wind went to the north-west, so the schooner was in a lee shore. However, Uncle William and MacNair let go the other anchor, and stowed the yards on deck and lowered the top mast. The anchor held and the ship was saved, although at one time it looked as if she would drag her anchors and become a wreck. Father arrived the next day to announce my birth during the night. There was not much delay after that and they resumed their voyage to the East Coast.

Father, of course, acted as mate in the schooner, as he had no education: but he could sign his name. He was extremely proud of that. I know little of this period as I was too young to remember anything much but just remember going aboard the schooner *"Alpha"* in Loch Toscaig when about five years old. Father was most of the time away in the schooner. In fact he told me that he was for 30 years at sea every winter trading round the British Isles, going south as far as Seville in Spain and going north as far as Iceland.

I really don't remember anything about conditions in the village and our home between 1884 and 1890 but now and again older people have told me a few stories about myself and my likeness to my Grandfather William. My father would be away at sea during this period and my Mother did the croft and ran the whole place. My grandmother (father's mother) and her unmarried daughter Ann, lived upstairs. My brother, Roderick, was born in 1886. Uncle William was married in 1885 and there is a story about the schooner *"Alpha"* arriving in Liverpool, and he rushing up to the Post Office to see if there was a telegram from his wife, as her first-born child was due. The telegram, however, handed to him was for my father to say that Roderick was born. His own daughter, Jessie, was born three days afterwards. As the croft was a bit too much work for my mother to do and care for the children at the same time, she occasionally had a young girl in the house to help her for three or four months, during the summer and early autumn.

In the spring of 1891 I was sent to school, which was almost three miles away. We normally left the house at 8.30am with a piece of oatcake in our pockets for lunch. We ate it on the way to school and it was all eaten by the time we got the first break in school. We always called the break Playtime. I can't remember the exact time we got out of school but, for the young ones, I think it was between 2.30 and 3pm. Normally we dawdled on the way home, although we must have been pretty hungry. I think we must have had a good dinner when we got home. In the summer there would be plenty of fresh herring and other fresh fish, potatoes, bread and very often fresh butter and, of course, plenty of milk. I remember, on occasions, Mother buying rice and we would have rice and milk when the old potatoes went done after early June. Of coursc, the new potatoes would not be fit for eating till mid July or later.

The schoolmaster had a red beard; he was Matheson by name, but we called him Geordie. He, of course, had a pupil teacher, as they were called, either male or female to help him. The appointment was made on merit. Any boy or girl who had scholastic abilities above the average would be put in the job. Most boys, however, were only too anxious to get out of school and immediately they reached 14 years of age, or, very often, under that age, they left school, whether or not they had higher abilities than the average. None of us, of course, could speak English. The school was there to teach, and when we were out playing the schoolmaster would tell us to speak English in the Playtime, but nobody did, and some of the wild boys would defy the schoolmaster, and they were thrashed for not speaking English. I always thought this extremely unfair for, after all, neither the boys nor the girls could put two words of English together in their early years in school. There were, of course, some children who were bilingual. The gardener (MacCowan) at Applecross House could not speak Gaelic, nor could his wife, but all their children could speak both languages fluently.

The older boys were a frequent source of trouble to the schoolmaster. They were very wild now and again. I have seen him getting hold of them in their seats and hauling them out on the floor to be thrashed. They would hang on to the seats and he would lose his temper; but for the fact that the seats were bolted to the floors, boys, seats and all would have been out on the middle of the floor. They would be kept in for disobeying orders, but immediately he left the school for his house for afternoon tea, they would open the window and jump out and run home. The school, very often, was a tug of war, and looking back on it, I often wonder how any order came out of such chaos. The fact is that most of the boys did well later on in life and I could name a good few that did extraordinarily well later on, which shows that early education is not of such importance after all. If the schoolmaster, of course, had taken a different line in teaching perhaps less of the tawse and the bamboo cane, it would have had a better effect on his scholars.

I was under the Pupil Teacher for a couple of years, a Miss McClure. Her father was working about the Big House and was also the Elder in the Church of Scotland. It was called by all the inhabitants of Applecross the Big Moderate Church and very few people worshipped there. Of course, the Gentry, (as they were called), and all who resided in the Big House during the shooting season, went to the Moderate Church.

About 1893-1894 the schooner *"Alpha"* was sold for £800 to Welshmen. She was lost several years afterwards with all hands. The price received for the schooner was divided in the family in the following manner; £300 each to Uncle William and Father; £200 to Grandmother and Aunt Ann, Father's unmarried sister. I think I have said already that her hands were very badly deformed, through my Father and her sister Mary, who were supposed to be looking after her when she was a child while their mother was working outside on the croft, allowing her too near the fire so that she fell into it. I once asked my Father why they sold the schooner. He said that coastal freights were very low for some years, through competition from the steamers, and they were barely making a living out of the whole business. There were other causes really, the main one being that, after young men from the village had been serving in her for several months, there was whispering that ghosts were seen in her and very often the main boom was banging about for no apparent cause. These rumours reached the Women, as my Father called his Wife and three Sisters, and every time he got home they were at him to get rid of the schooner before disaster overtook them at sea. I don't think my Father was really superstitious, for I never heard him say that he was frightened of any ghosts, even of the one the whole village believed in.

On one occasion while on a passage from Seville in Spain to Iceland with salt, the schooner got into a terrific gale of wind a few days before reaching Iceland. She started leaking very badly with the heavy pounding she was receiving, and the pumps could not be worked, as the salt somewhere had got into the bilges and the pump-rose. Father got down into the hold of the schooner with a shovel and made a tunnel under the pyramid of salt in the hold to the pump-rose and cleared it and through his action saved the schooner. Someone said (one of the crew, really) that if the salt had dropped on him, while he was in the tunnel, he would have been buried alive.

They in the schooner had, of course, narrow escapes, winter after winter trading on the coast. Anyway, the schooner was sold, ghosts and all, and my father was sorry for the Welshmen who lost their lives in her. The sea (or the bottom of the sea) is called Davy Jones' locker as so many Welshmen were drowned year in and year out.

My brother Roderick, was coming to school with me about these years. He is very like the MacLennans - tall (about 6 feet), good natured, but wild in school; able to run as fast as a hare and with enormous endurance. The schoolmaster used to tell him that he would do nothing better in this world than go about with a stick over his shoulders and a red handkerchief on the end of it; in other words the badge of the tramp. Roderick, however, went to sea, and was in command of cargo ships for 16 years and of a passenger ship for 14 years before retiring.

About those years, too, I was always collared by the old folk of Toscaig to bring them tobacco, sugar, tea, etc., from the shop (the merchant in Camusterrach was married to my Aunt). Roderick and the other boys would not wait for me, with the result that it took me about half an hour to catch up with them. In the summer time on our way home from school we nearly always had a bathe at the Camman, where there was a pool of sea water (fresh if the tide was out and it had been filled from the stream). As we only wore shorts, shirts and jackets we flung them off in a few seconds. On one occasion I remember the girls in the village coming home from school were behind us and when they saw our clothes on the side of the road they took them with them. We chased them with stones and in due course they were running off, yelling and dropping our garments: a simple life in those far-off days, but we never had a spite at the girls afterwards

* * *

I begin my story again - still at sea, but in the "Pendennis Castle" now instead of the "Southern Cross". Before going, or rather getting, into Durban, we had an S.O.S. from a Swedish ship to say that her Chief Engineer was seriously ill, so we changed course to go to her assistance, some 150 miles, which delayed our getting into Durban till 11am instead of 6am. The poor engineer died with double pneumonia. He rallied on board for the first few hours, but could not sustain it. After Durban we went to Johannesburg to see Proby's cousins. Her two aunts were married near there, at Randfontein. One, Mrs. Paterson, had a family of three children. There are now seven grandchildren, all grown up and some of them married. Proby's aunt, Mrs. MacKenzie, had no family. After spending a fortnight there we took a train to Cape Town, meeting relations there also, one a second cousin of Proby and the other a grandchild of Mrs. Paterson, now married. After spending a few days in Cape Town we boarded this ship for home.

* * *

CHAPTER THREE

Now to begin my real tale. We had a happy childhood in Toscaig. Father had a fishing boat of his own called the *"Sarah"*, but did not keep it very long as his partners were inclined to be a crabbed pair and one of them was rather lazy. So when he got a chance to join the Beatons' boat as a partner he sold the *"Sarah"*.

We boys went to school, except in the spring time, when one of us had to stay at home for a fortnight at potato planting. The potatoes were planted with the cas-chrom, a spade-like instrument, but much easier to dig with, as one does not bend so much. Father worked the cas-chrom and I followed him putting the potatoes in the row, and also seaweed, sometimes with a mixture of cow dung. Mother would be busy carrying some of the seaweed in a creel on her back and also the cow manure. Also Mother cut the potatoes for planting. In those days it would be the height of extravagance to put down or plant a full potato as seed. One potato was carefully examined and cut into small pieces according to the number of eyes that looked good for planting. I think the mixture of seaweed and cow manure must have been good manure for growing the potatoes, for invariably, we got a good crop. One year I remember there was an extremely good crop and we picked up in October 60 creels. A creel of potatoes was often more than a cwt. Creels were not made to a uniform size. Stronger families had bigger creels made for them, but usually they conformed to a pattern of one size for the women. Women in those days used them mostly and they were seldom seen without a creel of some commodity on their backs.

At this time (in thinking it over) we were very happy. My brother John, was born in 1890, Murdo in 1892 and Kenneth in 1894. Roderick and I were kept out of school when potato planting was on and again when peat cutting or drying was on. But neither of these things were as important as the spring work. We had a servant when any of the family were born in the summer or autumn. She generally arrived on term day in May and stayed with us for six months and she was paid £3 and her food during the six months period. Usually, she was a big, hefty woman and she had to be, for her work was normally doing the outside work and weeding potatoes, carrying peats in a creel and cutting the corn and hay with a sickle. After the spring work finished about the end of April, work was almost immediately begun on the peat cutting, especially if the weather was dry. This was hard work. Father first cut the topmost layer of the moss and rubbish with the caber. It was generally very sharp and it was pushed when holding two handles on each side with great force and one's belly did most of the pushing. Anyway, after the top layer of moss was removed one got down to the peat. The peat was cut with a "torsgian", a knife-like instrument with a sharp blade, with a right-angled piece which cut the peat into oblong pieces about a foot long and 4 inches wide on each side. We boys used to like peat cutting for it really meant a picnic all day. We left home after the cows were milked and breakfast over - taking the cows with us. We left for the moor and stayed there all day, Father cutting the peats and we laying them on the moor to dry. After they were dried, which normally took several days, we made little stacks of them. In reality we upended them, several supporting each other and they remained in that condition till they were stacked for the winter. This was done with a slanting roof and built up not unlike the roof of a house. And there they remained till they were needed for winter fuel. Our peats were cut on each side of Loch Toscaig, and when we required fuel we went and took them in creels to the shore, where we loaded them into our boat. When the tide came in the boat came almost up to the door of our shed and it was easy loading them into the shed with the minimum of labour. When peat cutting, peat lifting, stacking or boating them home, we went out for the whole day - in other words, if the weather was favourable, we seldom got home before 7pm, in time for supper and bed for tired boys. On one occasion, when father, mother and his sister Ann were bringing peats home in a boat, the plug came out and after a bit of searching it could not be found; so Father made his sister Ann plug up the plughole with her thumb. Father and Mother rowed the boat and Ann kept her thumb in the hole till they got home and Father got a bit of cork. Another time my mother and her sister-in-law took the boat to go and fetch peats. The men were either away at the fishing or then in the schooner. They rowed to the place where the peats were stored on the lochside, but they found the boat very heavy to row. Then when they got near the shore it completely stuck and they could not get near the storage place. On further investigation they discovered the anchor was never lifted and that was why the boat refused completely to go any further.

The sheep were put off the arable land about the middle of May. That was a great day for us boys. The sheep had to be sent up to the hill and all the gates around the fences and Galloway dykes had to be kept closed till the middle of October. In those days the village employed a shepherd, whose business it was to see that the sheep did not come into the corn, grass or potatoes; and very often we boys had to see that the cows, when let out in the mornings, or after their arrival at night, did not go into the corn or potatoes. By the way, the shepherd's pay was £3 for 6 months, and his food. He lived with the crofters. Those that had small crofts (or rather half crofts) kept him for a week and those with a full croft for a fortnight.

My grandmother died in 1897 or it may have been early 1898, she was 93. Her daughter Mary (Aunt Mary) said she was only between 91 and 92. Anyway we were always told that her youngest child was born when she was 53, but Aunt Mary thought she was a year or 18 months younger. I remember her very well. She was never sick in her life and had to work free for the MacKenzies of Applecross for 14 days every year when she was a young woman. Aunt Mary told me that she often said that she was in better health in Toscaig than she was in Uags, where she was born and brought up. She was over 40 before coming to Toscaig. Some men met her when she was about 90 carrying a creel of peats home without shoes on and only rough stockings (they were called mogan in Gaelic). He said to her that it was a shame her going out to take peats home and her sons shipowners. She saw nothing shameful about it and carrying fuel home at her age was quite a noble thing to do, she told him. One of the village women came in to see her a day or two before she died and she told her that her life now just seemed like coming up and down stairs.

Many people who live in towns will invariably ask, 'However did you pass the time in those remote villages?' Life, of course, was simple. There were lots of children, large families were the order of the day; so there must have been from 15 to 20 children in those days going to school from Toscaig alone. After school children were expected to, and did, help with the work on the croft. Nevertheless, we had plenty of time to play, especially in the summer months when, for three months, darkness did not come till 11pm. In the winter time children went to Ceilidh Houses where some one present sang songs and told stories, which nearly always included ghost stories, which frightened me a great deal. In the winter months also the women worked hard at carding and spinning and made all sorts of garments by knitting. They very often carded and spun the wool from their own sheep. I remember the Old Weaver very well. He made blankets and cloth. He was a character. His name was MacLeod and he was a very old man when I was a boy. With his death went the looms out of the district. He lived in Coillegillie and his loom was at the end of the house in a shed. He was supposed to be the greatest walker, by far, in the district, or even further into the other parishes. One time he had to go to see my grandmother about something when she lived in Uags, about 4 miles away. I am not sure but I think his name was Kenneth. My grandmother asked him to stay for dinner, 'The potatoes are on the boil.'

'No, no, Jessie,' said he, 'I put my own potatoes on when I left home and unless I hurry back they will be overboiled.'

Just imagine a man walking 8 miles while a pot of potatoes boiled. Another time he left Dingwall early in the morning, was in Coillegillie for dinner and walked after that to Lonbain, North Applecross, almost 20 miles both ways, and had his supper there. He went to the East coast fishing when things were slack in the weaving industry. He was travelling home (walking) one day with another Applecross man. They put up after supper at Achanalt. The weaver went to sleep immediately while his friend was having a smoke. He hardly got his pipe down when the weaver woke up. 'Come on, Roderick,' he said, 'it is time we were on the road.'

'God bless me,' said Roderick, 'I have not closed my eyes yet.'

There were no alarm clocks or clocks of any kind in those days so when the weaver went to bed he made a point of not relieving himself, so therefore, he woke up early and was very often on the road before the others got a wink of sleep.

In the years I am writing about, that is from about 1893 to 1900, if I remember rightly, I was going to school till 1898, but I don't remember when I left school; it would be, likely, after the examinations were over in July 1889. On the other hand I may have left school six months earlier. I know that I must have been going at least two or three seasons to the loch fishing from June to August-September. It depended on the herring fishing in the loch and that we got holidays from school from about the middle of July till nearly the end of August (6 weeks in all). These were our holidays from school during the whole year. The loch herring fishing was done, or rather carried out, by the Bodachs (the Gaelic for old men). When the men were approaching the 80s they were getting too old to go out in the fishing boats, which in those days went as far south as Loch Fyne and as far north as Stornoway; indeed if there were herring anywhere south of Cape Wrath in the numerous lochs skirting the West Coast, they would go there. Herring was so abundant in those days the good fishing was almost confined to the lochs around Skye - west and east, Loch Hourn and Loch Nevis were favourite lochs for good herring. In Toscaig, in those days, there were several old men who had handy boats (but not decked) with a mast and oars, and, of course, they had nets of their own. The nets were set in the loch late in the evenings and hauled in early in the mornings. We boys used to be very sleepy getting up at about 3am. If we got herring we would go to Kyleakin. The railway was not built in those days. If there were good signs of herring in the loch before setting the nets, the Bodachs would not go home to sleep; so we often went and slept on heather in a cave by the loch. Good signs for herring were sea gulls in great commotion, terns, gannets and other sea birds about the loch. My first trip to Kyleakin, after getting several crans one night in the loch, was with William Kennedy and Murdo MacKenzie, and when we got to the pier, I was so interested in my surroundings that, instead of filling the baskets with herrings, my eyes were on the folk coming and going on the ferry; so when William and Murdo would arrive back with the empty basket from the curing yard I would not have the other basket full. William shouted at me not to mind the girls and to attend to my work. William was a cousin of my Father. Another time we were crossing to Kyleakin with herring in the open boat and the sail set.

The boat was heeling over to the gunwale and Murdo, who was steering said to me to bail the boat. Used as I was to sailing boats, I was a wee bit frightened, so put the water out of the bailer on the weather side. Murdo, who was a very kindly man, said, 'Hoots, boy, put the water over the lee side, so as not to hit me in the face, and rest assured we have the boat well under control.'

By the time I was 14 years of age I was going out occasionally in the big fishing boats, if one of the members of the crew had to stay ashore for any reason. The reason was very often that a baby was due, and the man had to stay ashore for at least a couple of weeks, especially in the harvest months. Women, when having a baby, were normally at their usual work within a fortnight of the birth of the baby. My Father was very proud of his wife because she was never more than 10 days away from the harvest work. I once asked my Mother how did she manage to do the cutting of the corn with a sickle when I was only eight months. She replied that she brought an old blanket with her to the field and put it on the lee side of a stook of corn and that I was quite happy, and if I was hungry she fed me there and then.

To get back to the fishing boats, I remember on one occasion going with Father, Murdo Beaton and his son, Norman (he was younger than I was) to Loch Hourn in their fishing boat *"Mary Mactavish"*. Murdo's brother, Donald, had to stay at home to do the harvest. This *"Mary Mactavish"*, like all the other fishing boats of the day was only covered with a deck about a third of her length of 25 feet. We slept there and we cooked there, that is, under the deck. She was a sailing boat and had oars, but they were used only in a dead calm. Loch Hourn is the squalliest loch on the West Coast, except perhaps Loch Torridon. Murdo Beaton did the steering and was, of course, a fine seaman. One night we had to go for shelter under Eilean Pibroch, as it was too stormy to set the nets. The sails could be reefed to 5 reefs (it may have been 4) but in any case the sail was then very small. The boat had also a storm jib and a larger jib. It puzzles me even to this day how very few accidents took place in Loch Hourn because furious squalls hit it hard. If, of course, the squalls became furious there was always a man standing by the mainsail halyards, and there was nothing else doing, not even cooking, when there was danger. I think the fishermen really sensed the squalls and were always on the alert. My Father told me that while sheltering in Loch Slapin (it was even worse than the other two lochs I have mentioned for squalls) he saw the sea gulls flying and, taken off their guard, smashed against the cliffs in heavy squalls. I forgot to mention that Loch Hourn means in Gaelic Loch Hell and that Loch Nevis, further south, means Loch Heaven. Loch Nevis is very mountainous also, so I am unable to say why this loch should have a heavenly name. It may be the contours of the hills on the lochside.

To get back to my trip in the *"Mary Mactavish"*, we had not a very successful trip, but salted sufficient herring for the winter use of all the families. Loch Hourn herring was famous for curing.

For the year or two before leaving and after I had left school, my mother used to ask me to go and help "The Widow", a Mrs. Kennedy; in the Highlands in those days the widows had a hard life to bear. I really don't know how long she was a widow but her two daughters were married by this time. My Father was a second cousin of the widow's late husband and my mother was a cousin of the widow. Her maiden name was MacLennan. Although I could read and write English at this time I could not speak it to any extent. Mother, of course, pooh-poohed all this and said it was our business to look after all widows, especially Mrs. Kennedy, of whom my mother was very fond. The widow had a shop. She would tell me in Gaelic what to say to her supplier of goods in Glasgow. She always began by saying in Gaelic, 'Tell them that we are all well, and I hope they are all keeping well. The harvest is promising.' Or, if in the spring or summer, that the crops were beginning to show well, or looking well, etc. She would begin her order of sugar, paraffin, butter, etc. She kept her accounts by having a stroke for a shilling and a short stroke for sixpence and a dot for a penny. She, of course, could not read or write.

I often had to go to Kyle of Lochalsh (or earlier on to Kyleakin, before the train came to Kyle of Lochalsh) for goods for the widow. An old man, called John MacDonald, was often in charge. He was the man who looked after the road in Applecross and so he could take any day off which suited him. The widow was not a very popular woman with the fishermen, as they thought she was not lucky. I don't know why this should be, but I presume that, she being much more intelligent than most of the folk in the village, they assumed she had supernatural powers. When her goods arrived, my brother, Roderick, and I had to go and help her to get them up to her shop, which was just a small closet off the kitchen and about 500 yards from the shore. One time when we were playing with the other children a few yards from her house and we heard that a boat arrived with her groceries, we both decided we would hide. We got to our own house when snow was falling and went straight upstairs and hid ourselves under the bed. Within a quarter of an hour the widow arrived and we heard her telling Mother she needed the boys' help as it was snowing. My Mother told her that we were playing up at her own house. 'No,' she said, 'I followed their footsteps all the way down and they are in the house.' It did not take Mother long to get us.

Old John MacDonald, known as Shon, gave up the fishing after a frightening night near Loch Laxford or Lochinver. Two of his crew were in another boat helping them, when a north-west gale came away like a bolt out of the blue. All boats made for shelter but Shon was alone. He steered her through the gale, but could not leave the helm to take sail off her. Then he got in the shelter of the loch and drove her ashore on a sandy beach and when he took his sou'wester off all his hair also came out.

* * *

I am now at Loch Carron again; so will resume my story.

* * *

Village life in Toscaig in the years between 1895 and 1900 had many attractions. There were large families and many children to play with and, as often happened, work with. Schooling was, of course, compulsory, but the spring and harvest work were of most importance. When I left school the winter nights were often spent in listening to people singing Gaelic songs and telling old stories. Our own house was one of the houses where people came to Ceilidh, and we listened to stories from the old sailors and fishermen and, of course, to ghost stories. No evening was complete without a ghost story.

There was an old sailor in Toscaig, then a big powerful man - John MacKenzie - who had stopped wandering and settled down in the village with his brother and two sisters and, of course, bought his own fishing boat. I heard him telling a story about a sailing ship he was in, loading sugar in Javanese ports. In those days there were few harbours in Java and on the North Coast the sea is very shallow for about 10 miles in some places. One day, John MacKenzie and a sailor from Skye, who was also very tall and big, were taking the Captain ashore in one of the ship's boats. The Captain was a martinet and hated aboard the ship. The Skyeman was steering the small boat and he and John noticed a squall approaching, a common occurrence in Java. One of them said to the other in Gaelic, 'Let us drown the skipper as he has been starving us for months. We are both powerful swimmers and can easily reach the shore.' Just then the squall hit the small boat and over it went. The Skyeman should have really luffed her into the wind but neglected to do so. The Captain was a big man, well over six feet, and when the swimmers looked back, there was the Captain walking ashore. He really thought the capsize was a pure accident, so nothing was ever said about it.

Then there is the story about the Bodach Beag, the Gaelic for little old man. He appeared to people at the Camman, a valley between Toscaig and Culduie. I used to be very frightened of him, so never went alone after 8pm in the dark winter months. An old man from Toscaig once left in the early morning about 5am with a letter which he was anxious to go by the post which left Applecross at 8am. The letter was to his son who was sailing in a big sailing ship. When the father, carrying the letter, was approaching the Camman, a little man started to walk alongside of him; he was dressed in oilskins. The old man took no notice of him and in due course the little man disappeared under a culvert. I knew this man, Gillanders by name. He was over eighty when I was a boy, and he often took me along with him when fishing in the loch for herring. He was a very religious man. Anyway, the ship carrying his son went missing and his son was lost. They never heard when or where the ship was lost. There were other stories about the Bodach Beag which were told by unreliable people, so are not worth repeating.

In 1913 when I was home on leave from a ship, which I brought home after the Captain took ill in Rio de Janeiro, I was invited to tea by my cousins, Mary Ann and Jessie MacDonald. A Miss MacIver was also there. She was the second teacher in Applecross School at that time. On my way home (my cousins were in Upper Toscaig and we lived in Lower Toscaig) I told her that I would see her home to Culduie. About 10pm we set off and had, of course, to pass the dreadful Camman. Now I had to repass it on my way home. Gillies, the man of the house, must have noticed that I was not keen to go back alone and so he offered to walk back with me which I gladly accepted. He, of course, turned back after we passed the Camman. I was so ashamed of myself that I told my Mother what had happened. She said, 'William, the Bodach Beag has not been seen in Applecross since Lord Middleton (who was proprietor of Applecross) decided to do away with the pub in Applecross,' that was about 1880. My mother was a very practical woman, but I myself am not certain but what the Bodach Beag is still hovering around in the early hours of the morning at the Camman.

My brother John was never frightened of him. On one occasion he was walking home very late and when he got to the Bodach Beag's little cave he felt something going about his feet. He naturally got a start, but had the presence of mind to see for himself what this animal, natural or unnatural, was which was going around his feet; he lit a match and found a stray cairn terrier. Most men, of course, would have run as fast as their legs would carry them.

For several winters, from early February, Father was one of the crew of four of a boat which went poaching from Aird-dhubh to Applecross Bay or to Sand Bay, which goes in after passing Cruachrie Point, the most northerly point of Applecross Bay. It was arduous work and if he made £4 for six weeks' fishing he thought he was doing well. On one occasion, the crew, or some of them, were walking home to Toscaig early on a wet and cold morning, when one of them thought they heard the gamekeepers chasing them. The more they ran the more the footsteps increased, until one of them discovered that the flaps on their own seaboots, hitting each other as they ran, were the cause of the commotion. Another night, Father was coming home and saw, a little bit from the house, a huge animal with huge horns; most men in the darkness would have run into the house, but not he. We boys had rigged two oars in the bows of a small boat, which had arrived after Father left the house for the night's fishing. Father had no fear of unnatural phenomena, or possibly he did not believe in them. By examining the boat he found there was nothing mysterious about the huge animal.

Another story my Father used to tell us was about when he was a young man and worked for several months in the Inverness-Aberdeen construction of the railway. On his way home, walking of course in those days, he was grabbed by the shoulder on a very dark night when passing through Coille Tharvie, near Garve, by a man, possibly two. Anyway, my father not being a big tall man, gave himself a twist; the robber lost his grip and so my Father scrambled down the edge of the river and got away. My Father carried his savings with him, being £6 for several winter months work. Coille Tharvie, in those days, was famous for the robberies which took place there. When listening to the old stories I often wondered why people passed through there on a dark night. I thought they had an enormous amount of courage.

This is a story about a famous Highland minister called Big Macrae, who was very strong. While walking through the wood Coille Tharvie, he was attacked by three people. He knocked the first one out, then the other two. He, of course, was annoyed at the way these robbers carried on during the winter months, so he robbed them and was able to get £6 off them. He carried on with his journey and in due course reached Achanalt Inn. In the Inn was a man bemoaning his fate - how was he going to keep his wife and family alive for the next few months. Big Macrae asked whatever had happened. So he told him his story and the way he was robbed earlier in the evening at Coille Tharvie.

'And how much did they take from you?' said Macrae.

'All my earnings for several months, in all, £6.'

'Here is your £6,' said Macrae, 'they tried to rob me but I robbed them.'

This great and powerful preacher, Big Macrae, was for a long while minister in the parish of Lochs, Lewis. He and another minister, Finlayson, were once going to a Communion in Skye, and a boat was sent for them to Lewis. Everything went alright at first, but then a storm arose, and as it was a head wind the Skyemen were struggling to make land before it got worse. Finlayson was getting frightened; so he said to the Skyemen that he would pray for a little while. 'You pray if you like,' said the oarsman, 'but let the big minister take an oar.'

Another time Macrae was having an evening walk with his chief elder. They talked about the topics of the day, but at last the chief elder said that they should be discussing religion and leave earthly things to others. Then Macrae picked up a dry stick from the side of the road and said to the elder that religion would become as dry as that stick if they discussed nothing else. On another occasion he was preaching below high water mark to a very large congregation just in front of where our house in Loch Carron now stands. The people of Loch Carron, at the time of the Disruption 1843, were all for the Free Church, and this happened a few years after. Naturally, the Established Minister was very much concerned about his own church becoming empty, and he was a good worthy minister; so he went along to where Macrae was preaching and tried to get the people to come back to his church. Nobody would go but he refused to leave. Big Macrae then said to him that when he was a young man he was a "brocair" (Gaelic for badger hunter) and when the badger could not do anything else, and was trapped, he put out a bad smell. The badgers in those days, were supposed to be bad for taking and attacking young lambs and the brocairs were the men who did away with the badgers. Actually, the general opinion nowadays is that the badgers are harmless creatures, and the culprit, even in those faraway days, was the fox.

A man, Donald Gordon, lived next door to us in Toscaig, but in 1905 a new house for the Kennedys was built between the two houses. Donald was a frequent visitor to our house, and was very superstitious, especially about ghosts and fairies. He told us once that his brother John went out poaching deer on a very bright, moonlit night near the Giant's Hill (Neas a'fhamhair), which goes up from the Camman (the habitation of the Bodach Beag). He saw a fine hind not very far away and he put up his gun to shoot her. When he got the sights of the gun on her and was ready to fire, he noticed that it was a woman he was firing at. He got such a fright that he threw the gun down and ran home and never even looked back. On arrival home he fainted and was perspiring and could not say a word. Anyway, he came round by next morning and went to fetch his gun. Where he was poaching was supposed to be where the last Giant in Scotland was killed. He was an enormous man. One afternoon he killed a large ox, carried it over his shoulders, set a fire under tripods of three large pieces of timber and made a good meal for himself. It being a very hot day he slept afterwards and when sound asleep one of the little men, a Pict, came over the edge of the Hill and shot him dead through the heart with his arrows.

Above our house in Toscaig were three green mounds called the Fairy Hills. Donald Gordon told me once, that a man carrying a keg of whisky was walking near the Fairy Hills in the twilight on or about the New Year. The fairies came out of the hills and made a fuss and danced about and around him and, before he knew where he was, he was inside with the fairies and he stayed with them for a year to the day.

There were two sisters staying near us in a small house. The elder sister was very religious and often visited my grandmother and conversed with her on religion. Her sister had been ailing most of her life, if not the whole of her life. It was said that the fairies took the real child away and left the ailing one shortly after she was born, around the New Year's Eve.

When my Uncle Norman (my Mother's brother) was a boy about 12, he was very friendly with a boy whom these old women were bringing up. The old women (indeed they were not so very old then) had an axe in the house, which few houses in those days possessed. The boys were going to cut shinty clubs, but knew they would be refused the axe if they asked for it. So they planned to lift it during family morning worship. Norman arrived as the women and the boy were having their breakfast. After breakfast, when the family prayers came on, Norman went on his knees near where he knew the axe was kept. The prayers were going on in the normal way and just before they ended the woman conducting them shouted, 'Martha, Martha, the axe, the axe,' and Martha grabbed the axe just before Norman got it. 'Amen' was never said after these prayers.

My mother told me a story about a very religious woman. Her name was Macrae. She told her next door neighbour, also a devout woman, that she had heard a woman in the village passing at the back of her house, wailing and weeping a few nights before. Not long after that, a man and his boy and girl were gathering seaweed in Crowlin Island. On the way home the boat capsized and the boy and girl were drowned. When the mother, who was at home, heard the news, that was the route she took when she went to meet her husband, who was saved.

While on this subject, I must tell another story about a man who was sent from Kintail to Applecross. The Lord Seaforth arrived at Eilean Donan Castle (this was well over 200 years ago) and whilst there he was anxious to send word to his fellow clansmen, the MacKenzies of Applecross. He sent his message with one of his staff, a MacKenzie, a big, powerful man. It being winter, the man took the shortest route and arrived over in good time, and marched back over Bealach-Nam-Bo. While he was marching up to the top there came on a blizzard and he lost his way and fell over the cliffs of Sgurr a'Chaorachain. As he did not arrive back in Kintail when expected, scouts were sent out to look for him. They came over the hill above Duncraig, opposite Plockton, and got down to the village. All the men there were away fishing and so were all the boats, except one which was full of water. They overturned it and dumped the water out and launched it. This boat had never been launched for, when the builder completed it, a woman came along and said she saw the body of a fine-looking man stretched out on the floor boards. The Kintail men did not know the story, so took the boat to Russel on the Applecross shore and went searching for the messenger. In due course they found his body and took it down and laid it on the floor boards of the boat. After that nobody was frightened to sail in the boat.

* * *

Aunt Ann, my Father's sister, went to Oban in the early winter of 1898. Her mother died (that is, our grandmother) some time before, at the age of 91 or 93. Nobody was very certain of her age. Uncle William was now settled in Oban. The yacht, *"Aster"*, of which he was master, was laid up for the season there. The yacht was in commission, as a rule, from late March till early November. It was a great day for Aunt Ann when she left for Oban to visit her brother. Roderick and I were longing for her to come back to hear her stories and adventures. She had never been away from Applecross except short trips to the neighbouring parishes at communion time. The day Aunt Ann arrived back we boys could hardly contain ourselves till we got her to sit down at the fire to tell us the story. Father happened to be in and sitting on the other side of the fire and he was listening to her, but a bit incredulous, I suppose, at first. The story began when Aunt Ann was ferried over to Kyleakin, where she joined the Glasgow steamer *"Claymore"*, which ran regularly from Glasgow to Sutherland, once a week. Between her and her sister ship, the *"Clansman"*, a bi-weekly service was maintained. A steerage passage to Glasgow was 8/- and only 4/- to Oban. The *"Claymore"* of course went into all the little villages and ports going south, and also called in at the Island of Eigg and, although she left Kyleakin at 4am, she did not get to Oban till 4pm. From there she sailed direct to Glasgow.

In those days every passenger on the *"Claymore"* going ashore at Tobermory, Mull, had to pay 1d for pier dues. One Skyeman was going ashore with his friend when the demand for the 1d was made at the gate. Everybody resented this demand and the Skyemen were refusing to pay, but the law was, no money, no passage. At last in desperation the Skyemen said, 'I have a load on my back, will the cost be the same?'

'Yes,' said the gatesman, 'you can take on your back as much as you can carry.'

So instantly the friend jumped on his back and he was carried through free.

Aunt Ann had been able to see the saloon and the good food which the first class passengers were eating, but as she was steerage she had nothing to eat but dry biscuits for a 12 hour journey. She took a long while to tell us her story, and I suppose Father was getting irritated at her frivolous stories to us. At last he said to us and his sister, 'Woman, I have known dozens of people who have been round Cape Horn several times, but you seem to gather more information and news in your trip of 12 hours, than they did in years of voyaging.'

In those days, most of the men who lived in the villages of Camusteel, Milton and Shore Street which were near the Big House, as Applecross House was called, got work in the gardens of the big house or on the big farm connected with it. In fact they lived contentedly there on a very small wage; but they had their crofts, of course. Their families had to go south for work - boys and girls. The girls always went in to service. Just about this time people started talking about weekends, and going here and there for weekends. Of course there was no equivalent word in Gaelic, which was the language that every one spoke. One day two old men were talking about their families and those of them who were in service in the south.

'Yes,' said one of the old men. 'We got a letter from Mary yesterday.'

'And how is she?' said the other.

'Oh, she is fine and is going away on the weekend.'

'Weekend?' said the other. 'What is that?'

'I don't know,' said he, 'unless it is a big steamer that runs between Glasgow and Oban!'

In those far away days I think the people were fairly happy, although they had not much of this world's goods. They had to scratch a living out of their crofts and fishing. Going to church was the order of the day, every Sunday, and there were no conveyances except one's legs; almost every Sunday my Father walked the distance (nearly three miles) to church. He walked twice every Sunday, to morning and evening services. Mother also very often did the two services but she, on the other hand, stayed with friends or our relations near the Church and had dinner with them. The minister normally took 2½ hours to preach and complete the service and consequently some of the old people, especially the old men, were tired as they were at the fishing the whole week, rowing the boats or sailing them. The hardest work of all was pulling the nets at daylight, sometimes twice a night, if there were no signs of herrings by 1am.

The minister of Applecross, in those days, was Kenneth MacDonald, a native of the Parish, so had a lot of relations in the villages. One Sunday he was expounding the Gospels and I think the subject was on covetousness, and he was giving an example of how the people in Applecross were covetous of the people in Torridon because the land there was supposed to be more fertile than Applecross and could support three cows to the acre to two in Applecross. One of his own relations (a fisherman) went to sleep during the long sermon and just woke up in time to hear about the cows.

'Lies, lies, lies,' he said. 'Applecross is a far better place for cows than Torridon.'

People in the villages seldom left their homes unless shortage of cash sent them to look for work in the south. Every year there were Communions in all the Parishes, normally from the end of May to the end of September and these were so arranged that the services never clashed. The great popular preachers were present at the services, so the people, if at all possible, flocked from one parish to another every few weeks. The Applecross people went to Loch Carron, Plockton, Ardelve, Kintail, Raasay, Gairloch and further afield in open boats and sometimes, of course, walking. As I said already, there were famous ministers in those days who preached the Gospels very forcefully. Very often it was damnation and hell and the terrors and torments for those who did not believe. It is said that on one occasion, while preaching at a Communion service in Loch Carron, a minister, who was well known in the Highlands, was beginning his sermon when he noticed a woman whom he knew well, holding an umbrella above her to keep the strong sun off her head. He shouted, 'Take that umbrella down.'

No response from the woman. He repeated the same words again, but again, no response.

At last he shouted, 'Margaret, take that umbrella down and do not try to preserve the beauty that God never gave you.'

The umbrella was taken down.

The churches, in those days, were far too small to hold the concourse of people who travelled for miles to the Communions; so the services were conducted in small valleys with sloping sides, so that the folk could sit on the grass. To understand the distances walked, my uncle in Kinlochewe told me that he remembered people leaving Kinlochewe (walking) at midnight to be in time in Applecross for the first service at 11am on Sunday, about 30 miles.

CHAPTER FOUR

Now I must come to my own career. After I left school, I was more or less employed working the croft and going out in fishing boats to relieve somcone or other. Also very often I went out fishing with other boys, and by these means I may have earned about £5 a year, which was by no means to be sneezed at in those days when money was of great value. "Breaking" into a £1 note was gravely considered and was not encouraged unless something or other was drastically needed. "Breaking into a £1 note" is a literal translation from the Gaelic.

In November 1899 my Father went to Oban to visit my Uncle William who, as I mentioned already, was captain of a yacht called the *"Aster"*. The owner's name was Evans, from Derby. His father was a banker; Evan's Bank it was called, and it was about this time, or earlier, taken over by one of the big London banks. Evans leased the Estate of Jura from the Campbells of Jura. It was a good estate for sport and my Uncle (as I mentioned already), John Murchison - no relation, but the husband of my mother's sister, Jessie - was the head gamekeeper for the estate. The year, however, that I joined the yacht, this Uncle retired to Kinlochewe, where he leased a sheep farm called Coulin. Well, to get back to November 1899, Father spent about three weeks in Oban and when he arrived back he brought the good news that I was to join the yacht as ordinary seaman in the early spring, wages £2 a month - and I was to pay for my own food. My Father also brought another precious bundle, a box of tools. Uncle William's father-in-law was a joiner and he had died some months before and so Uncle gave a large number of his tools to Father. Father really was never a handy man with tools. He was a great expert on mending or making nets. The joiner's tools were a great asset for my brother Roderick and me. He was more adept with them than I and one of his first achievements was to make the stock of a gun; on this he secured a very long cartridge and so, by boring a small hole in the inward end, he was able to place a small bit of powder on top of the hole when the cartridge was loaded. When all was ready a match was lighted and, lo and behold, the gun was fired and the little pellets reached the target. It is a wonder we were not killed, but the whole invention was so tidy that it was harmless. Probably Mother got hold of the gun in due course and dealt with it, by either destroying it or hiding it or making firewood of it. The winter as usual went past quickly. On fine days we went fishing to catch gurnets. The sea between Raasay and Applecross was just alive with them and it was common for us to catch between 500 and 800 with four hooks on a short winter's day. The bait was a piece of a gurnet. Another job I had to do was to bring peats home in a creel. These were about a mile away. Roderick was still in school. We normally had a good stock of peats at home for winter use, for most of our peats were cut and stored on the south side of the loch and not very far from the sea. Therefore, when the harvest was secured and the herring fishing came to an end in November, Father and I (or Father without me) would go away for the day - to take peats down to the shore of the loch in creels. The days were short but on a good day one man would carry about eight creel loads to the shore of the loch and there stack them till he had a large boat load. Then, when the spring tides came, we would go and fetch them. The rest was easy. On spring tides the sea came up to within a few feet of our byre, where the peats were again stacked for winter use.

The cows occupied the other end of the byre and, of course, the hens another section. Father was never very fond of the hens. He maintained that they ate too much corn, oats really, for all the benefit mankind got out of them. His favourite food was fish, either salted or fresh. When he was a young man, oats were used for making oatmeal which was also one of Father's good foods. Again in his young days there was an oatmeal mill in practically every parish in the Highlands, indeed in many villages. I remember myself when several crofters in Applecross sent their oats to the mill in Milton to be made into meal. In one year when I was a boy, Duncan Kennedy got six bolls of meal from his croft. The remains of the mill are still there and parts of the wheel that gave the power to grind the oats into meal. The large wheel got its power from the loch above the mill and when we boys looked at this wheel when the water was turned on, we were fascinated. Today the water power turns the blades of a turbine and gives us electricity. It still amazes me whenever I think of the 1890's, how people reared large, healthy families on so little with so much effort. They certainly worked hard, and maintained the crofts in good heart by manuring then with seaweed and dung. I have no doubt but the land lacked certain elements, but nevertheless, the yields of oats and potatoes were not too bad. When I was over in Applecross the other day, October 1960, the crofts were derelict and only a crop of hay to feed a few cows and a few bags of potatoes. The houses are much better nowadays, but the population consists of mostly old people pensioned or assisted by the Government. A way of life has perished, but it is doubtful if the people are happier.

* * *

This is the year 1960 and the 2nd day of the month of December. I must admit I have done very little work, if any, on this work of mine, since we arrived back from New Zealand, Australia and South Africa.

* * *

Well, to get back to my early days in Applecross, the winter of 1899 and 1900 was more or less like other winters. There was a bit of a stir about the Boer War in South Africa, but as there were no daily papers and perhaps only one or two weekly papers, news was scant. Furthermore, it was a war run by professional soldiers and therefore the general opinion of the villagers was that they were paid to do the job. The days when the Highlanders went to war with the Chiefs had ended with Culloden. I don't think any of the villagers volunteered to go to the South African War. As I have already said they were all either sailors or fishermen. The Navy was not involved, so there was really no extra recruitment of seafaring people. Again there is the old Gaelic saying, 'Little wars far away kept up the price of fish and cattle.'

By early March I was packing up to join the yacht *"Aster"* which was laid up in Oban for the winter months. My mother was getting my clothes ready. She always saw that a bible was put into my sailor's bag. Father was not much concerned about my departure. He had done the same old job himself from the time he was 11 and he was now 62 years old. My cousin Murdo MacDonald (he was chief Cook of the yacht) and I were ferried across to Kyle of Lochalsh in the usual way by sailing boat or oars when there was a calm. This would be about the middle or towards the end of March, 1900. The boat for Oban - called either the *"Claymore"* or *"Clansman"* - left Kyle of Lochalsh either on Tuesdays or Fridays and got to Oban the same day at 4pm after many calls on the way. The fare was 8/- steerage. There was a raffle on board by the steerage passengers and I won a melodeon. Useless, really, to me as I could not play one note on any musical instrument; however, it became very useful on the yacht as the red headed cabin boy could play it very well and it was therefore in great demand after our usual chores were completed at about 6pm. We stayed in Uncle's house for the night and next morning we were ferried to the yacht and work for me started in earnest. I know I felt the time very long working from 6am till about 6pm. I sometimes thought the time would never pass. There were no stated hours when working in the village. Some days, if the weather was good and work had to be done, we worked till 8 or 9pm, but then if rain came on and no work could be done outside, we had an easy time.

The yacht had to be got ready for sea. Within a week this was accomplished and we sailed for Greenock, calling at Jura on the way. There I met my Uncle and Aunt Jessie, but they were preparing to leave in May. I, of course, was sorry, for my Aunt would have been of help to me in the summer. We sailed the next day for Greenock and docked there alongside of Caird's Shipbuilding Yard, where the repairs were carried out and we were busy cleaning and scraping. In due course we entered dry dock and there the finishing touches were put on the yacht, so we sailed for Rhu, near Helensburgh, where a large number of the Clyde yachts were being fitted out. It amazes me now, if I try to understand what kept six or seven sailors so busy for almost two months. Most of it, I suppose, unnecessary work, but yachts had to be spick and span, so all the old varnish had to be taken off the bulwarks, boats, etc, as they were made of teak wood. Sometime in May everything was shining and we sailed for Jura where we awaited the arrival of Mr. Evans. We normally picked him and his party up in West Loch Tarbert and took them over to Jura to stay for a short time in the Lodge there. When I was in Greenock, I bought a sea cutter's hat or cap with two brass buttons in it. I was very proud of it. We were paid fortnightly and I sent whatever money was over to my Father and Mother; that is after I paid for food, etc. When I bought the cap, which cost a few shillings, explanations had to be made why my remittance was not so big. Our uniform was supplied by the owner, normally a working jersey and a good one for going ashore and two pairs of blue trousers and seamen's caps, round ones with a little tassel coming down over one ear. On the jersey was written *"S.Y. Aster"*, so I quite fancied myself in my go-ashore uniform. How easy it was in those days to satisfy the whims of the teenagers. The teenagers of these days get more money in a day than I got in a week and they don't seen to be very happy. The only difference really is that we had to work very hard and had little time for leisure. Nowadays, they get both too much leisure and have far too much money to spend. During our short stay in Jura, before starting our cruises, we had to water and store the yacht. The water had to be brought out by one of the boats in small casks from the burn that ran down from the hills. It took us more than a day to fill our large tanks ashore. It was a pleasant job on a summer's day.

Now the yacht was ready for cruising, so the party, usually from six to ten, came aboard and we were on the way to visit the lochs and islands of the West of Scotland, and our first port of call was Oban for coaling. Sometimes we went beforehand to Oban to get our bunkers aboard. The bay of Oban in those days was full of yachts, ranging in size from very large steam ones to small sailing ones. Boats of all sizes, rushing back and forward, but they were mostly rowing boats as motor launches were unknown and steam pinnaces were few and far between. Some of the very large yachts carried their own steam launches. What a busy place Oban was in those days - and it was people of wealth that went there for holidays.

Now our cruise started in earnest and we called and stayed for the night in any loch or fairly good harbour which was available before 6pm. I suppose the owner preferred to dine when the yacht was at anchor. This first cruise of the season was a long one and we went as far north as the Shetland Isles. Mr. Evans, I believe, was a bit of a naturalist, for he was keenly interested in all the sea birds. On the way south on this cruise we called at St. Kilda and, of course, the whole of the population was so interested in Mr. Evans and the *"Aster"*. It was also a help for the natives and the English parties that my Uncle William was a fluent Gaelic speaker. Naturally he was the interpreter. I specially remember an old man named MacQueen, if my memory does not fail me, who was the "star turn" at the interviews. As a professor from Oxford was on board as a guest, who, presumably, was a naturalist, the conversation was mostly about sea birds and the few land birds that stayed the whole year around St. Kilda. MacQueen must have been nearly 90 years old then, so the Professor was asking him questions about the Great Auk, which was killed by the natives of St. Kilda. Now I cannot be certain whether MacQueen was at the killing of this bird or was told the story by his father. It has been proved that this bird killed by the St. Kildans was the last of the species, so naturally the professor was very interested in the story. According to MacQueen, this huge bird came to St. Kilda and the people got very frightened and thought the Devil himself had come to visit them. After a conference it was decided that there was only one thing to do and that was to kill the monster. They set to and in no time the deed was done. I can't remember the details of the bird given by MacQueen to the professor, but I suppose he wrote them all down and they are now preserved in some museum in Great Britain.

Before we came to anchor in the Bay of St Kilda, we cruised round the west of the Islands. The main Island cliffs facing the west are about 1,000 feet high and perpendicular indeed at the top sloping outwards slightly. The cliffs are full of gannets; there must be thousands there in the summer months and it was a great sight when we blew the yacht's whistle close in to the cliffs and nearly all the birds took to their wings. The professor was so impressed that he made up his mind to climb up after dinner and see the birds from the top. This was arranged by my uncle and the professor, Uncle and a native began the climb from the Bay. Everything went on famously till they reached the top of the western cliffs. The St. Kildan walked on to the very edge and looked down in much the same manner as anyone looks down from his own doorstep. My uncle was a step or two behind him, for he really was not afraid of heights being an old sailor. The St. Kildan looked back only to see the professor on his hands and knees and coming forward in a very gingerly way.

The native looked so surprised at this man on his knees that he exclaimed in Gaelic to my uncle and in astonishment said, 'Whatever is the matter with the man? Is he frightened?'

The Professor did not get near the edge of the cliff, but nevertheless was anxious to know what the St. Kildan was saying. Very irritably he said to my uncle, 'What is he saying, Captain, tell me?'

'Well, Professor,' said my uncle, 'he is merely asking if you are frightened.'

'Yes, yes! Tell him,' the Professor shouted, 'and for the life of me I cannot go forward another inch.'

The St. Kildans, of course, were used to heights and climbing, for their main work in the autumn months was hunting and catching young birds which they salted down for their winter food, and they could only be obtained by going up and down the cliffs at very great risk, and sometimes their sheep went into all sorts of places especially on the neighbouring islands and great risks had to be taken to save them from falling into the sea.

We stayed a night or two in St. Kilda as the place was of great interest to the owner and the guests, and as long as the wind did not blow from an easterly direction, the Captain was quite happy in the Bay. We called at Barra, Rhum, etc, on the way back to Jura.

Immediately on our arrival back at the buoy at Jura, we sailors were kept busy fitting out, watering, etc, for the next cruise. We, of course, did not keep an anchor watch when at the buoy, but normally we worked from 6am till 5.30 or 6pm. I suppose it appeared to me so unnecessary in those days to be permanently scrubbing, cleaning and polishing a ship and keeping people employed for practically 12 hours a day at such work and for the pleasure of a few men and women, but we were paid for it and that was the basis of everybody's philosophy in those days. It was all so different from the fishing boats at home. They were, of course, kept decently clean, but their main purpose was to make money for the people who manned them and indeed, looking back on that period, their heavy labour was often unrewarded and if they finished up with cash amounting to between

£20 and £30 a season after all bills were paid, they considered they were lucky.

What I did not like about yachting was keeping watch when cruising and up all day. I suppose I was a sleepy young man and to this day I regret the amount of sleep I lost in those days. Anyway, when all was ready and spick and span, we went over to West Loch Tarbert to pick up more gentry, as we called them. They would come by train from the south to Gourock and then by boat to East Tarbert and coach to the West Loch. After a rest at the Castle we set sail for the north again. We never went sailing south or to Ireland, but again visited the Lochs and Islands of the West, and again to Orkney and Shetland. On one of the cruises we called at Applecross (Loch Toscaig) and stayed the night, so I got home. By mid August the yacht was more or less laid up except for runs to West Loch Tarbert for the Gentry coming deer shooting and runs to Oban for bunkering.

About early September we had to go for a fortnight or three weeks to Loch Tarbert on the west coast of Jura. A very isolated place, but a sheltered place and good anchorage and good for all sorts of fishing. The East Coast of Jura was not a good fishing place, except cuddies. During our stay in Loch Tarbert the owner and parties occupied a shooting lodge at the bottom of the Paps of Jura and I seem to remember that there is a lovely sandy beach there. The lodge was built there and was in a bay before entering Loch Tarbert, West Jura. On the whole it was a pleasant interlude, although there were no villages or crofts on the West of Jura. Really a barren, dreary place. When we got back to the moorings opposite the Castle there was not much to do, although we sailors were not idle, especially me, who was in charge of the dinghy. Someone wanted to go ashore or come aboard - and I was the young man that attended to them. In early October or late September we left the moorings and went to the harbour of the Small Isles a couple of miles from the Castle and opposite the village where the buoy was. Just opposite the Castle was an open bay. Although a small island was at the mouth of the bay, it gave little shelter and when the October gales came thundering in, the bay was not a good harbour, so that was the reason we left it. The Small Isles, on the other hand, is a perfect harbour, with a narrow entrance. We seldom moved out of this anchorage the whole of

October, but the sailors were kept busy and besides kept an anchorage watch as, presumably, the Insurance Company demanded it. Towards the end of the month preparations were being made for the owner and the last of his parties to leave for the south, so the yacht was busy for a few days transporting themselves and their luggage to West Loch Tarbert where they found the usual transports for the south. The yacht than sailed for Oban where she was laid up for the season. It normally took about a week or ten days and I and the other Applecross men then took the steamer to Kyle of Lochalsh, where the pier had been completed and the steamer could come alongside. Also the Stornoway steamer had begun calling in at Applecross a few years before, so it was not isolated and it was easy to get there every afternoon by steamer, but it was not so easy to get away as the steamer left at 3am and for us Toscaig boys it was a long walk of five miles in the middle of the night, carrying a sailor's bag on our shoulders. Normally then we preferred being ferried to Kyle of Lochalsh when going south.

During the winter months in Applecross there was much to do. On fine days we went fishing, mostly gurnets. The sea was alive with them in those days and they generally came near to the surface in good days and one fished them by lines with a bit of themselves as bait. I occasionally went out in one of the fishing boats, if one of the crew took a week off, but by the end of November the local large herring fishing boats were laid up for the winter months. There was also fuel (peats) to bring home and this was done by carrying them in creels on one's back all through bogs, stones, and narrow paths and this work could only be done in decent weather. A good stack of peats had to be stored in a shed or, if there was room, in the byre; it would be a grievous error to get short of fuel during bad weather. Peat was the only source of warmth for the house and no cooking could be done without peats. In other words, peat took the place in the house where today we have coal, electricity, paraffin, oil heaters and gas which comes to the door in cylinders. Furthermore, the oatmeal and flour came to the house in 140lb bags and was either taken on men's backs, or in a barrow from the shop nearly three miles away. In spite of all these drawbacks, the houses were warm and cosy and the baking and cooking was done very efficiently. In those days and during the whole of the winter months the women were always either spinning, carding or making woollen wear. I remember the women doing the waulking, that was cleaning and stretching the cloth when it came from the local weaver. They sang special songs when working at it. This reminds me of a story about Roderick and me when we were about 10 and 8 years old. Our barn then was in Upper Toscaig - Mother's Father's old barn - so Roderick and I were sent to the barn every Saturday to bring a week's supply of hay down for the cows which were in the byre in Lower Toscaig. Our barn was up on a brae so one day we started rolling large stones down the brae and they hit large iron containers at the back of a thatched cottage. The noise brought out the old woman and her daughter and they made a fearful row. We naturally ran away. We found out later on that the iron containers and tubs contained human urine which was preserved for cleaning new blankets and tweeds. Presumably it was used then for the same purpose as ammonia is used for nowadays.

In those days the long Highland winter never appeared to us young men as lonely or in any way dull. People very often went to Ceilidhs and usually to a special house where old stories were told and Gaelic songs sung. I don't think a newspaper was coming to the village of Toscaig. I myself was one of the first to get a weekly paper, as everyone was then so interested in the Boer War. As so few people could read or write in those days, especially the old people, the news had to be translated. The winter then passed quickly and by early March 1901 I was again getting ready for the yacht which we joined in Oban in late March. The same old crew, and I was still an ordinary seaman, but I think I got a few shillings more in my pay.

We went through the same performance, getting the yacht ready for going round to Greenock where alterations were made, especially to the deck houses, which improved her appearance a good deal. The extensions and height added to the fore and aft houses gave much more rooms to the Captain, officers and engineers and to the owner and his guests, but the crew's quarters remained as they were. The hammocks were permanently lashed to the side of the forecastle and the table was across the forecastle with benches on each side of it. The lavatory was at the sharp end of the forecastle. It really wasn't too uncomfortable, but a bit too small for twelve people. The routine after the repairs was the same as the year before, that is, we went to an anchorage in Rhu and began the scraping, sand-papering and varnishing of everything. She was, of course, dry docked and painted in Greenock in Cairds' yard before we left there.

There were quite a lot of bad people, men and women, in those days at the entrance to Cairds' Shipbuilding Yard. I was disgusted at the drunkenness and loose morals of men and women at the corners of the streets leading in to the yard. Indeed I was often frightened of them, but no-one could come to much harm as it was bright in the evening till very late. In due course the yacht was spick and span for another season and we went to our old quarters in June to await the owner and his guests.

There is no point in going over the cruises again to the Shetland Islands and all round the Orkneys and, of course, the various lochs on the mainland and the Islands on the West Coast. I remember on one occasion staying for the night at the Shiant Isles. There is a good anchorage open to the eastward and quite sheltered unless the wind came strong from the east or north-east. On this trip Sir A. Geikie (afterwards Lord Geikie) was aboard. No sooner had we dropped the anchor than I was ordered to take him ashore. He was then famous as one of the greatest geologists in the country and was probably one of the leading geologists in the world. We were on the beach in no time and he always carried a small canvas bag and hammers and he was in no time breaking bits of stones here and there. All of a sudden he came on a smallish, round stone and got quite excited over it, while he was carefully examining it. He did not put it into the bag with the others, but carried it in his hand. The Captain was at the gangway when we arrived back at the yacht and the salutation my uncle got was to have a good look at the stone.

Very gravely Geikie said to my uncle, 'God alone knows how this stone got to this island.'

My uncle was a very religious man, so said to Geikie, 'It is me that is happy to hear you mention God.'

Sir A. Geikie said, 'I hope I haven't conveyed to you in all our talks that I did not believe in God, for I always believed in God.'

Sir A. Geikie, when he started as a young man, was under Sir Roderick Murchison and they tramped the Highlands on numerous occasions together and, of course, he became a great friend of my

Uncle's all the years he was aboard the yacht as a guest. Probably the name Murchison made a difference in their friendship; Sir A. Geikie wrote the life of Sir Roderick Murchison in two volumes. Anyway, Geikie and Uncle had many long, serious talks and very often about geology when Sir A. Geikie would talk quite enthusiastically about millions of years ago, which was quite beyond Uncle's comprehension of the universe as he was taught and understood it. He was a regular guest in the yacht for years on our various cruises and was a very nice, jovial little man as I remember him. He wrote a large number of books on geology, but, for the layman, his book on his reminiscences is delightful to read, and it is full of stories about the Highlands. He is a bit too severe on the Highlanders and their ways and that they appeared to be dreamy and lazy. His work was really ashore amongst the rocks and hills, whereas in those days most of the men on the West Coast and the Islands got their livelihood out of the sea, out for most of the week in small, uncomfortable, undecked boats, setting nets at nightfall and lifting them at daybreak. Rowing if there was no wind to the nearest herring curing station, no wonder they appeared lazy to the southern tourists when they were perhaps loafing around the village. If a fisherman was standing at his house with his hands in his pockets, it was very likely because he was earning a deserved rest from his toils of night and day in storms and calm. When Sir A. Geikie was a young man, he worked for three years on a Geological Survey of Skye and the small islands off its shore. He lived in Broadford, but in the summer months camped in a tent on the Island of Pabay just a little distance off the shore. He was known to the people of Skye as Bodachan na Creag - "The old man of the rocks". On one occasion he was gathering stones on the shores of Loch Slapin and he had two hefty Skyemen with him to carry the stones back to his hotel in Broadford in his usual strong canvas bags. It came on a storm of wind and rain so he told the Skyemen that he would hurry on home and when they got to Broadford they could leave the bags of stones at the hotel. They talked things over between themselves and came to the wise conclusion (as they thought) that to carry stones for miles and miles from Loch Slapin to Broadford was a sheer waste of time. They there and then dumped all the stones on the side of the road, walked quite gleefully to Broadford and filled the bags with stones from the shore at Broadford Bay, and deposited them in the hotel as they were told. One can imagine Sir A. Geikie's disgusted look at his valuable stones having so carelessly been dealt with by the lazy Skyemen. Perhaps one should sympathise with him when he has a "dig" at the lazy Highlandman.

He was once on a walking tour with Sir R. Murchison (I should really say on a working tour) in the Highlands, and they put up for the weekend in Torridon. Geikie was then a very young man, so he decided on Sunday morning to go for a climb on the high hills. It was a beautiful day so, presumably, he was in no hurry getting back, but when it began to get dark at about 11pm, Sir Roderick began worrying about him as he had not put in an appearance. He told the people in the household and their neighbours to organise a search party. They all refused as they maintained it was still the Sabbath and would be wicked to hunt for a man who, for his own pleasure, went mountain climbing on the Sabbath. Anyway, Sir Roderick fussed, so by 1am they were ready to go as it was now Monday morning, but just then young Geikie arrived back and was surprised at all the fuss about his disappearance.

* * *

I now must get back to the yacht and the usual routine which differed little from year to year. We did the usual cruises before the deer shooting began in August and there is hardly a loch from Jura northwards on the mainland and in the islands I did not visit during my term in the yacht. My uncle was a great authority on the Scottish Coast. He, of course, gained his experience in their own schooners from the time he was 15 years old. He was indeed a great navigator of the lochs of the Highlands and Islands. Once we stayed for the night in Loch Hourn almost at the very end on Loch Skiary. It is very tricky getting in there and we had to almost shave the rocks in some places. The owner was expecting Lady Burton to visit him the next day. Lord and Lady Burton's estate was at Loch Quoich several miles from the end of Loch Hourn. I was sent ashore to the old gamekeeper to get news and also, I presume, to try and get milk.

I was talking to the gamekeeper when all of a sudden he said, 'You have a lovely singer aboard the yacht and it was so calm last night that her voice was so beautiful here as it must have been on the yacht. I imagine,' he said, 'she is as beautiful herself as her voice, but could not make her out at all although I had my telescope on you for a long time.'

'That singing you heard was a gramophone,' I said.

'A gramophone?' he said. 'Is he alive or what?'

'No,' said I. 'It is a box.'

'Come, come!' he said. 'That was a woman and could not have been a box.' He had never heard of a gramophone. The conversation was in Gaelic and it was not so easy to explain.

The deer shooting started in August as usual and we were on our usual routine. We left the yacht for the season in November and I seem to remember that this year we did not take the direct boat home. We went by boat to Fort William, thence train for Mallaig and mail steamer to Kyle of Lochalsh. This would be about the time that the construction of the railway line to Mallaig was completed. It is possible I am making a mistake and that it was the following year we went home that way. It was, in any case, of great interest to us. The winter at home was just a repeat of other winters and the only diversion was a trip with Mother to Kinlochewe to see Aunt Jessie (Mother's sister). Just to show the difficulties of getting away from Applecross in those days, we got ferried on a fishing boat in the afternoon, stayed the night in the station in the waiting room and took the morning train to Achnasheen and walked the 10 miles from there to Kinlochewe. We called at a gamekeeper's house where there were friends of Aunt Jessie and had tea with them.

Although Aunt Jessie was hard in money matters, she was gracious in her own house, but very commanding and forthright in her speech. When Uncle John and Aunt Jessie retired from Jura where he was gamekeeper with Mr. Evans, they went in with his brother Kenneth and his daughter's house. But Uncle John built an extension of two large rooms for himself and his wife so that they had quite a large house for the family and visitors. Uncle John took me over to see the Kinlochewe Bard; I think his name was MacKenzie. He was a very old man then and he sang to us a few of his own Gaelic songs.

Actually he was not considered a great or even a good Bard and he was very sarcastic, with rather a good dose of rough language. We enjoyed our trip there and it was my first visit to a place where I could not see the sea. Loch Maree was only two miles away but it is a freshwater loch. A steamer ran on it during the summer months for tourists.

Uncle John told me a good story about his shepherd's (Mr. Cross's) grandfather. I may have mentioned already that Uncle John took over on lease the sheep farm of Coulin six miles away and Mr. Cross, the shepherd, lived in the house in Coulin attached to the farm. To get back to Cross's grandfather - I am not certain but it was his great-grandfather - he was, I believe, the first Post to carry letters from Achnasheen, which was at that time a stage coach stop from Dingwall and the south. There was not a road between Gairloch and Poolewe or Achnasheen in those days. The Isle of Lewis packet sailing boat carried mails and passengers to Stornoway from Poolewe. John Cross, as I said, was the postman and he had to carry the mailbag on his back to Poolewe from Achnasheen and the path in those days went on the east side of the loch, very rough and full of boulders. There were only stepping stones to cross the rivers, John walked the distance of 30 miles summer and winter three times a week without complaints. Agitation got up in the Island of Lewis that the mails were very irregular and complaints were sent to the Head Post Office in Edinburgh, and one of the causes was pinpointed in John. John was a very tall, finely built man with enormous strength, so he answered the complaints by asking the Post Office to send someone up to examine the road. At last the Post Office in Edinburgh agreed. When John Cross saw a weak-kneed individual coming off the stage coach, he had doubts if the man could ever get to Poolewe. However, they set off on their long walk and they were not far away when it started to rain, with a strong wind and the Edinburgh man was getting tired, and in the end collapsed altogether. John put the man on his back and arrived with him and the mail bag at his destination tired, but none the worse for his journey. After a good night's rest the man returned to Edinburgh and there were no further complaints. By the way, I gathered that the mail of those days consisted of a few letters.

CHAPTER FIVE

Another year began - 1902 - and Uncle William wrote to say that Mr. Evans was still in the Glasgow Central Hotel very ill and unable to get home to Derby. He was attended by Sir William MacEwen. Eventually Mr. Evans got home, but there were doubts if he would recover sufficiently to get up to the Highlands or put the yacht under commission. I was not really worrying very much and was beginning to think that it was time I started in earnest a seafaring life and got into foreign going ships and got my time in quicker as I had by then made up my mind to get out of the forecastle on to the quarterdeck. Uncle William wrote again in March and there was still doubt about the yacht going into commission, but Sir William was going to Derby shortly and then it would be decided whether the yacht would be fitted out or not. My father and especially my mother were anxious I should stay at home to help with the spring work. Father never had any qualms about his family going to sea. The sea gave him a good life and probably a hard one, but that did not bother him. Anyway, I decided to stay at home till the end of April, but early in April a telegram came to say that I was to join the yacht the following week. This was a month later than usual so most of the fitting out was done in Oban and we went in due course to Greenock for dry docking. Sir William MacEwen put two and two together and decided that Mr. Evans would get over his illness and that the yacht would be a good place for him to convalesce in. When we got the yacht spick and span we went to Liverpool to pick up himself and one or two of his friends, but he was no longer fit to engage in deer shooting. He spent a great part of this summer about the Clyde and when Mr. Evans bought a house in Ascog, Bute, we never after that wandered so far away. Again I went home for the winter months, although by now I was growing concerned about getting to sea in foreign service ships. Again in March I was asked to rejoin the yacht and Uncle William said that the coming season would be spent in foreign countries, especially the Norwegian fjords. This would suit me as I would get full time in for the certificate I was hoping to get some day. The dreams of the owner did not mature, so we did not get away from the Scottish coast after all. Probably he did not feel well enough to take long voyages. By this time Jura was given up; presumably the lease of it expired, and we were based in Ascog, which was not a good anchorage in an easterly wind. Many a time we had to heave up anchor and go to Rothesay bay for shelter. About the end of October Mr. Evans went south to Derby and we went to Oban to lay up at the usual buoy. I thought now that it was time I cut the painter so, instead of going home, I took the train to Glasgow and went to the Sailors' Home on the Broomielaw. It was in a rough vicinity, but, nevertheless, it was a handy place for a young man looking for a ship. The accommodation was good and as far as I remember the food was decent. Pretty rough, I suppose, but then sailors of those days were used to rough things and took for granted the conditions prevailing at the time.

It was in the spring of this year or the next that a very sad drowning accident happened in Toscaig. A man, Kenneth MacRae, his daughter aged 18 and his son, about 14 years old, were gathering seaweed on the island of Crowlin for manure for the croft. They left the harbour with a full load of seaweed and set the sail to get into Loch Toscaig. They were getting along fairly well and the father was steering. He was an old sailor. It is not certain whether the boat was overloaded or a sudden gust of wind capsized the boat but they were all thrown into the water. My brother Roderick and John MacKenzie were not far away in a small rowing boat and at once went to their assistance. They rescued the father, but the girl was dead before they got her out of the water. I can't remember if the boy was ever found. It cast a terrible gloom over the village and after that there was less seaweed taken ashore for manuring the crofts and, by 1921, after the First World War, none was gathered.

When I arrived in Glasgow about the end of October, I began hunting for a berth in any ship. Finally I signed on in the S.S. *"Columbia"*, the Anchor Line passenger ship running between Glasgow and New York and I had to be aboard at 6am the following day. I marched down the Broomielaw at 5.30am to be aboard at the correct time. The Broomielaw had a very bad reputation in those days, but no-one molested me. It seems so strange to me now that in those days, while when in Applecross I was only afraid of ghosts and would be very scared coming past the Camman (between Culduie and

Toscaig) on dark winter nights, yet it never occurred to me that any human being would do me any harm, but here now in a large, presumably civilised city, I was scared stiff that a few men would attack me and steal my sailor's bag, my only big asset. I was no sooner aboard than I was asked to turn to and get the decks washed. Passengers were due to arrive on board at about noon. While I was washing the decks down, the Bosun's mate was holding the hose with an enormous pressure of water in it; a woman came aboard and started arguing with the Bosun's mate. The argument went on for a little while and then he shouted, 'Boys, give the hose a lift.' And he chased the woman ashore with a heavy spout of water at her heels. Someone said that she was his wife and he was going away for another voyage without giving her any money. Sailors in those days were anything but thrifty, at least the majority of them. On the other hand there was a quartermaster from the north coast of Applecross for years in the *"Columbia"*, and he had a good wife and two children, and their house was open to all Applecross people. His wife kept a lodger and they were very comfortable as far as I know.

In less than three weeks we were back in Glasgow, so I left the ship. Short voyages did not suit my book, for any time for a certificate only counted for the time I spent at sea. Now I was looking for another ship and this time for a longer voyage. I was not long in the Sailors' Home when I signed on in a ship called the *"Otterspool"*, bound for the Mediterranean.

I saw something not far from the docks which so disgusted me that I have never forgotten it. One evening I was walking home from the south side of Princess dock and was opposite a pub when I noticed that a man was pulling a woman out by the hair of her head. She was yelling, but someone said that the man came home from work, found the house empty and his wife in the pub. My uncle William, who was master of the yacht *"Aster"* was a strict teetotaller, so it never occurred to me to have strong drink and in any case there were no pubs in Applecross in my day. I used to go into pubs with sailors, but always had soft drinks, but once I took beer to try it, and the taste was so awful that I never tried it again. The same with smoking. I did not like it when I saw the woman being pulled out of the pub; I said to myself that drink was obviously bad for people, so I became a teetotaller and non-smoker. Drinking and smoking were just a habit and did not do any good to anyone, furthermore it was a waste of money.

We left Glasgow for Italy (Genoa) with a cargo of coal and on discharging it we sailed for a small island in the Ionian sea to load iron ore. It was a small island with only the people in the mine working there. We had to put into another island, Syra, I believe the name was, to get permission to load and go through Customs, etc. We were not very long there when we were fully loaded and I remember the 2nd mate pointing out to me another island and he said that was where St. John was imprisoned. We set sail for Tripoli, North Africa, to take more cargo aboard. It was Esparto Grass and we filled the holds with it on top of the iron ore. In those days there was no harbour in Tripoli. It was a roadstead, with a tiny harbour where the lighters were loaded. It was not easy loading there as a ground swell was continually coming into the Bay.

I should have told a story about the S.S. *"Columbia"* earlier on. When in New York, I was on a stage over the side of the ship painting the hull.

The Chief Officer peered over and noticed that my companion hadn't a shirt on, so he shouted to him, 'Where is your shirt?'

The sailor replied, 'I have only one and I had to wash it last night, sir.'

I bought presents for home and Aunt Jessie in New York. I can't remember what I got for home, but the one Aunt Jessie got was a large, old-fashioned album, covered with velvet, which she greatly appreciated.

To get back to the *"Otterspool"*. When the loading of the cargo was completed and the Captain ready to go ashore to sign the usual papers, he ordered us to get the boat ready to take him ashore. We swung the boat over the side and I jumped into the forward end and another man into the stern sheets. All of a sudden the forward falls gave way and I and the other man fell head forward into the sea and the boat was upended with the after falls holding her. I swam about for a little while and caught a rope and so did the other man and we were hauled aboard. We were none the worse for our ducking and the Captain ordered us a glass or "a tot", as sailors called it, of rum.

I don't suppose the boat falls were removed for years. Masters and mates were extremely careless about their own or other people's lives then and remained so till the First World War, when they were forced by the authorities and, of course, the Board of Trade to see that life-boats were seaworthy and boat drill attended to regularly. Also, in those days, long before the war, life jackets were put in boxes and there they remained for years on end without anyone even looking at them. Presumably inspections of sorts were carried out on passenger ships, but in tramps they were just another nuisance inflicted on poor sailors and extra work for the officers by the Board of Trade. Actually I believe that life jackets were unknown on board ships till the Board of Trade made a compulsory rule that every ship must have them aboard about the year 1894.

In due course we arrived back in Glasgow in the *"Otterspool"* and I was back in the Sailors' Home. One day the Welsh Captain of the *"Cambrian Chief"* (I am not sure of the name) came into the Sailors' Home looking for sailors for his big four-masted barque. I said I would go but, as she was not sailing for three weeks, I decided to go home. When I got home I forgot about the next ship and I was urged to stay at home much longer and help with the spring work. Life at home was very comfortable compared with life on the ocean waves and in any case I had been away for a year, so I stayed at home for six weeks. I was away again in April and was looking for a ship. Things were slack so, against my better judgement, I went for another trip to the Mediterranean. A small tramp, the *"Baron Huntly"*. An awful skipper, a Swede, who some way or other got a British certificate. Looking back on it now I suppose he, himself, was chased by the owners, hence his bullying. One stormy night, going across the Bay of Biscay, I was in the look out in the forecastle head. As heavy seas were beginning to come over the bows, I was called aft to the Bridge and told to keep the lookout from there. As the spray was coming over the bridge, I edged inwards to get into the shelter of the canvas dodger in front of the Bridge. Just then the Captain came up to the Bridge, saw me sheltering and pushed me away and said that this was for mates, not sailors. So I was again exposed to the elements. This was the only ship I was ever in where the canvas dodger did not stretch the whole breadth of the ship. Probably the canvas was, like other things, rationed. One voyage was enough so I left her on our return to the Clyde.

The *"Aster"* was fitting out in Rhu when I got to Glasgow and my brother Roderick was aboard for his first voyage to sea. I took a day off and went down to see them and, while talking to Uncle William, something was said about quartermasters and that it was a better life than in the forecastle. He there and then sent a letter to Captain Ovenstone who was a friend of his and an old Captain in the Anchor Line. He was then the shore captain to the shipbuilders Caird & Co, Greenock. He was responsible for new ships' trials, etc. Anyway, the first thing I knew I was quartermaster of the *"Anchoria"*, an old passenger ship, sailing between Glasgow and New York. I made three voyages in her, I was losing a lot of time between voyages, although I worked aboard while the ship was in Glasgow. I left her and joined the S.S. *"Irrawaddy"* as quartermaster, a passenger and cargo ship running to Rangoon. I made a voyage in her and by the time I got home another year almost passed, so I went home for another holiday. While I was at home I went over to Kishorn where my cousin Murdo Murchison was home from Australia. He had almost his time in for 2nd mate and was soon going to Glasgow to finish his time and take a voyage of six months' duration. We planned to go in the same ship. We were not very long looking for a ship when we obtained berths in a steamer called the S.S. *"Nairnshire"* for a voyage to Australia and New Zealand. We carried a large number of emigrants, although the ship was not specially fitted, but of course had all the essentials. The passage money was very low and that was a great consideration in those days. We went from Glasgow to Swansea and finally to Liverpool to complete loading. There was an old navy man lamptrimmer in this ship. He joined the ship in London. One day I asked him how he liked Glasgow.

'I never saw much of it,' he said, 'and never got past Doggy Watson's.' A pub near the docks.

Another day he nearly fell overboard in Swansea in March in very cold weather. He said, 'I would not mind being drowned in warm water, but I would hate it in this freezing weather.'

After we sailed we got very bad weather in the Bay of Biscay and one or two of the forecastle ports got smashed in. Before we got the carpenter down to shore them up, there were several feet of water in the forecastle. There was one fat sailor - his watch below - who lay in his bed till one big roll from the ship sent the water over his lower bunk and that made him jump out at once.

Our only call on the way out was Cape Town to take bunkers aboard. Those large ships of between 10,000 and 12,000 tons dead weight needed an enormous amount of coal to speed them along at over 12 knots per hour. We stowed coal in all sorts of corners and places to have sufficient to take us on to Sydney, calling at Adelaide and Melbourne on the way. Eventually we got to Sydney and that evening my Uncle Norman came on board and took myself and Murdo Murchison home to his house in Enfield. I saw a lot of him during our stay for the best part of a week, also his wife and two children. He left Applecross in the *"Alpha"* about 1877 and then took to deep sea sailing and eventually landed in Sydney and stayed there. He was the youngest of my mother's family. He sailed on the Australian coast, sat for his 2nd mate's certificate and got it. He sailed for a while as 2nd mate but decided to get a job ashore and joined the staff of Dalgetty & Co.

We had a very rough lot of firemen in the *"Nairnshire"*; while in Sydney some of them decided to take away the laundry van which was delivering the ship's washing just as they were going ashore. The van had two fiery horses and when the firemen got on to the van, the horses bolted and caused a sensation, racing through some parts of the town. The police caught them and they were fined or, failing payment, to go to prison the next day. Anyway, the Captain bailed them out and the police landed them aboard before we sailed for Auckland. When we got to Auckland they had another escapade. They went into a grocer's shop (the Captain would not give them money after the affair in Sydney) and said that they were sailors in a coasting vessel and needed stores - which really they meant to sell for the voyage.

The grocer got a bit suspicious and said, 'Oh, yes. Where does your ship sail to?'

The sailors, not knowing any ports either big or small in New Zealand, were at a disadvantage so at last said, 'Our coasting vessel goes to Rothesay and Millport.'

Naturally, the grocer said he would call the police and they, of course, leapt out of the shop.

I was charmed with Auckland and the weather was so warm we washed the decks down at noon on a Saturday in our bare feet and in less than three weeks we were in the Bluff, the south end of New Zealand, and to our surprise it came on a snow storm.

We got into Wellington which was our last port for discharging the Home Cargo. While there we went a lot to the Seamen's Mission where concerts, tea, etc, were given. It was in the charge of a Padre, who was a great teetotaller, and every one of us was asked to sign the Temperance Pledge and a number of the crew did so. To my amazement the old lamptrimmer signed it and got a certificate to that effect. Later on in Dunedin I saw the lamptrimmer enjoying his booze, so I said to him that he had signed the pledge not to drink any more.

'Of course,' he said. 'I signed it and I am proud of my certificate and it is framed and hanging above my bunk.'

From the Bluff, where it was blowing and very cold, we sailed for Hobart, Tasmania, where we loaded a large amount of apples, including a deck cargo. Nothing out of the way happened on the way to Durban, except that someone opened a case of apples on the main deck below the foremast and every sailor that went to the ladder to go on the lookout in the crow's nest stole an apple from the opened box. I got toothache on the way across, at least it felt like that for a couple of days, so I was advised to go to the Chief Engineer for he was an amateur dentist. I explained to him how I felt.

He looked at my teeth and said, 'I never saw such a fine set of teeth before, and whatever caused the pain, it is not toothache.'

He was right and so no further pain.

We arrived in Durban in the evening and orders were given to all hands that they were not allowed ashore. Evidently, great trouble was caused to the emigration officers then through sailors deserting their ships. Another sailor and I must have been working down the hold for we had not heard of the orders, or at least they were not conveyed to us properly, so, when we finished the job we were on, we walked ashore, purchased fruit, etc, and then got back on board. Large numbers of the firemen went ashore and defied the authorities. Later on the ship was searched and the police grabbed the other sailor and me and took us ashore and put us into jail. We protested, but it was no use and we were given a blanket and told to sleep on the concrete floor. In about an hour a policeman came into the cell and let us out. Word came from the Captain of the ship that we were to be sent back to the ship at once. About an hour in the cells was enough for me. The firemen, however, were not so lucky, for they were sent to work on the breakwater till we sailed in a couple of days.

In due course we got to Liverpool and were signed off and we took the train to Glasgow. Murdo went to school to study for his 2nd mate's certificate and I went home for a little holiday.

If I remember rightly, it was on this occasion that I happened to be at the post office when word came through that the House of Lords decided that all the property and funds of the United Free Church were to be handed over to the Free Church. The House of Lords' decision shook the United Free Church. Presumably, it was they that left the Free Church, so those remaining in the Free Church, a small minority, became entitled to vast properties and funds. As usual on my arrival in the house, Father asked what news from the "town". So I told the story of the decision of the House of Lords. Some people from Uags were in the house and they belonged to the Wee Frees as that Church was nicknamed. They took the news quite unemotionally and Father, who was a partner in their fishing boat, was not very disturbed either. They were all good friends and religion was not one of their strong points and would not disturb their conscience overmuch. The village of Uags was on the very southerly point of Applecross and there was no road to it; the easiest transport was by boat. Two brothers lived there with their large families. Today it is deserted. Shortly after the Uags folk left, a man from Culduie came in and Mother asked him to stay for supper. We informed him of the decision made by the House of Lords. He was an ardent United Free Church man. Well, he would not take this decision lying down. I said that there was no way out of it, although some lawyers contended that as the minority (some 50 ministers) could not be expected to administer the vast property and funds they had been awarded, an Act of Parliament should be passed to enable all concerned to be given justice. This is what actually happened in due course. The old man, however, got very angry over the affair, as there were only a few families in Applecross that remained loyal to the Free Church, about, I should say, less than 10% of the congregation. All through supper the argument went on and the old man harping on the fact that less than 10% of the people should inherit the church and manse. In the end he clinched his argument by saying that if that church was locked up by the minority, he would be the first man to cut down a large tree and smash the door in. Both congregations worshipped in the church at different hours till it eventually was handed over to the 90% of the people. I never stayed at home in those days. It was nice and comfortable compared to life on the ocean wave, but it was sea time that counted.

CHAPTER SIX

I am not sure if the following story took place when I was leaving home this time, or on an earlier departure. I was packing my bags in the kitchen as Mother was bringing all my odds and ends. She always saw a Bible was put in my bag. Just then Mairi Dhubh came in, one of the Tinker family, or a gypsy as they are called elsewhere. Mairi Dhubh was supposed to have the second sight and some cruel folk called her a witch. She tried to sell my mother a tin pail, but my mother kept on saying that she had too many already.

Then Mairi turned to me and said, 'Young man, I see you are going to sea.'

I said, 'Yes, but as there is a gale of southerly wind blowing, it is not likely that the men will be able to ferry me across to Kyle of Lochalsh tomorrow.'

She said, 'Buy the pail for one shilling and tomorrow will be a good day.'

Knowing Mairi's reputation since I was a child, I thought to myself that it wasn't costing me much to get a fine day tomorrow, so I bought the pail, much, I believe, against my mother's judgement. Tomorrow arrived and, behold, it was a lovely, calm day and the men that were to ferry me arrived at the house. Donald Gordon, our next door neighbour, was very superstitious and was one of the ferrymen. When we got to the shore everything was shipshape in the boat. Normally, when plans were made for ferrying, the boat would be half full of water, an oar would be missing, rowlocks could not be found, the sail would be in a cave, etc. After we cleared the loch a breeze of leading wind blew in from the east and we sailed right into Kyle. When the breeze sprang up, I told the men about my experience with Mairi Dhubh.

Donald Gordon said, 'Luck will follow you,' or words to that effect. 'It is good you bought the pail.'

I learnt afterwards that the boat got a fair wind going back and required no rowing which was strenuous in those days. I noticed years afterwards that the pail had not been used and when I approached Mother about it, she said that out of her good nature the Tinkers sold her too many pails, but one day my pail would no doubt become handy and useful.

As usual I went to the Sailor's Home and next day I was going round the docks looking for a ship. I thought, however, it was time I was going into sail, so I went aboard the *"Loch Broom"* which was loading for Adelaide and Melbourne. The mate, Kellyrack, I believe his name was, accepted my book and said they would be signing on in a few days. Although I was never in a square rigged ship, I was used to sailing boats from my boyhood. Unless I sailed in a square rigger, I could not sit for an exam that would enable me to be mate or master in all kinds of ship. If one served his time in a steamer, one's certificate was marked S.S., in other words Steamship, and if one served his time in a schooner, one got a certificate marked Fore and Aft only. I was signed on as A.B. (Able Bodied seaman). I really did not know much about a square rigged ship but I soon picked up the "ropes".

I left the sailor's home at 5.30am to be on board at 6am. As usual I was a bit scared going down the Broomielaw, but all went well. I went ashore at the breakfast hour to get my Donkey's Breakfast. I probably ordered it the day before. A Donkey's Breakfast was a sort of mattress filled with straw and cost a 1/- or 2/-.

In the afternoon we hauled out of the dock with the pilot aboard. The master was Captain Martin, known to all sailors as Bully Martin. He lived in Gourock and never took the ship down the river. The mate and pilot did that and anchored her at the Tail of the Bank. Most of the crew were drunk and in any case we could not sail from the Tail of the Bank till everyone was sober. Captain Martin is mentioned in one of Bone's books. Indeed there is a whole chapter to himself. Captain Bone was 2nd mate with him in the *"Loch Ness"*. I was in the mate's watch and therefore in the port forecastle. There was nothing in it but the bare bunks and the anchor cable through the hawse pipe which came into the forecastle. The hawse pipe was closed the best way we could, but the water came through it and swished out through the door. Once we were well away from land the cable was unshackled from the anchor and lowered into the chain locks and the hawse pipe was properly fitted with a wooden block and quite watertight.

To get back to the Tail of the Bank, I remember seeing the Mallaig trains passing outside Helensburgh and thinking how nice it would be to be homebound on one of them.

On the 7th November 1905 in the afternoon two tugs came alongside, one with the Captain and his two daughters, and the other to tow us out into the Atlantic. The anchor was hove short and the tow rope taken aboard the ocean tug. I was sent to the wheel and the anchor hoved up. The Captain's daughters and all our mails were put aboard the other tug. Captain Martin was walking up and down on the poop.

The daughters shouted to him, 'Goodbye, Daddie dear, you will get your hash now.'

He snorted back, 'Goodbye.' Hash is a popular dish with sailors and all the time the Captain was ashore, his hash was never made so good as aboard ship.

We were towed out to the North of Ireland, the tug was cast off, sail was set and away we went with a strong N.W. wind. It was a leading wind with all the sails set. I looked at the log trailing behind us one day when I was at the wheel and she was doing 15 knots. Bully Martin had the reputation for cracking on and when he got the chance he was never afraid to carry sail.

We were soon in fine weather and in the North East Trade winds and got to the Equator in 18 days, a remarkably good run. Some sailors even today do not believe that any clipper ship did the mileage claimed for them in 24 hours in their heyday, and my own cousin, Captain MacDonald, who was marine superintendent of Ellerman Bucknall & City Line, doubts very much if the *"Loch Broom"* did 15 knots per hour. He was also an officer and seaman in the Loch Line but few masters sailed their ships as hard as Bully Martin. There is a story about him when he was master of the *"Loch Ness"*. He had a bet on with the master of the *"Samuel Plimsoll"* on the voyage home from Melbourne. The *"Samuel Plimsoll"*'s owners were the well-known Aberdeen Line who also owned the *"Thermopylae"* which made a passage from the Lizard to Melbourne in 60 days. Anyway, the *"Loch Ness"* and the *"Samuel Plimsoll"* left about the same time. The *"Loch Ness"* carried passengers in those days. There were a couple of ministers aboard and as Bully Martin was cracking on and never taking sail in, the parsons in agreement with the other passengers went to the Captain and prayed to him to reduce sail.

'Get off my poop,' he roared at them.

A heavy squall hit the ship later on and put some of the masts overboard, so he had to put into the Falkland Isles under jury masts for repairs.

There is another story about him. When he was master of the woolclipper *"Benvenue"*, they were running the Easting down, that is between the Cape of Good Hope and New Zealand, with several hundred emigrants aboard. The gale was increasing in force with a very heavy sea behind them. He had two men at the wheel and he himself stood by conning the ship and keeping her right before the gale. A heavy sea came on board the poop (a sailor's term for it - she pooped) and carried the Captain and the two men on to the main deck and landed in the hencoop. That is the place the hens were carried on sailing ships. The mate who was near the mizzen rigging managed to grip the remains of a smashed wheel and when the ship recovered from the shock, the mate noticed that part of the wheel was gone. He, however, jumped to it and others came to help him and together they managed to keep the ship before the wind on her course. Later on the Captain and the two men appeared none the worse for their experience. The marvellous thing is that the ship did not broach to, in other words, that her head did not come into the wind without anyone at the wheel for some minutes. Had she broached to, she was bound to go under. Miracles often happened at sea, but no seaman would imagine that the ship would recover in view of the gale and the speed she was travelling at.

To begin again my story of the *"Loch Broom"*, we got into the south easterly trade wind in very good time and more or less escaped the doldrums, which are the calms between the north easterly and south easterly trade winds, and by Christmas Day we were sailing past Tristan da Cunha Island with a good breeze of north easterly wind. The tops of the mountains were covered with mist. We had plum pudding that day, the only day a sailor gets a pudding. Bully Martin fed us really very well according to the standards of the time. There is a story about some mean masters of sailing ships who told their cooks to open the galley skylight (which was always directly below the main yard) and put a basin on the floor below the skylight. The cook then was told to go up in the yard with a bag of currants and drop them into the bowl. Those that got into the bowl or basin went into the plum pudding but the currants that missed it were collected and kept for the following year's Christmas.

We did not go far south for the prevalent westerly winds. We got them in latitude 45°. We sighted the island of Kerguelen, but the steady westerlies took us into Adelaide in very good time. Our passage out was a very smart one, 72 days from the North of Ireland to Adelaide. It would be considered by any standards a very fine passage. I said that we did not go very far south. Old sailing ships' masters were often accused of pushing so far south that the sailors would be forced to buy clothes out of the slop chest. All sailing ships' masters carried slop chests, that is, under-clothing, socks, jerseys, oilskins, seaboots, tobacco, etc, and they were a Godsend to sailors who came aboard ships in what they stood up in. The price was just put against their pay. I heard stories about some masters who would be supervising the Chief Steward on Saturday nights when the slop chests were usually opened. If sales were not going very well when running the Easting down, the Captain would come up on the poop and order the course to be altered a few points more to the southward. By the following Saturday the weather would be so cold and bad that the sailors would have to buy warm extra clothing. Probably mythical stories, for sailors were always spinning yarns about ships and captains.

One night in Adelaide I got severe tummy pains, probably caused by going off salt food and onto fresh food. I complained to the mate and he gave me a dose of black draught. It was the great cure on sailing ships; even if one fell off the main yard and broke one's leg, the standard cure was a dose of black draught. Some of the sailors got drunk in Adelaide and as usual left the ship, but most if not all were collected and put on board for the trip to Melbourne. We sailed to Melbourne after the discharge of our Adelaide cargo and had a good passage and sailed up to Melbourne from Port Philip's Head. We grounded on a sand bank with all sails set and a pilot aboard, but floated off in a few hours' time. After discharge of our cargo, we were more or less laid up and quite a number of the crew were paid off. We were waiting for a wool cargo and did not begin loading till March and that was in a very leisurely manner. The Captain stayed ashore and only came down to see us for an hour to two every morning. We were always busy in port and one day another sailor and I were painting the bow and figurehead and the stage we were on was a bit rickety owing to the curvature of the bow. I was doing the white and he the black and very often we had to pass each other on the stage. I warned the other chap to hang on while I passed round him, but he did not and the shaky stage swung and we fell and were both in the dock swimming to the landing place in the wall of the dock. The mate came along and saw me swimming with a paint brush in one hand. He shouted to me not to lose the brush and that was all the sympathy we got. The other lad was told he would have to pay for the brush he lost. We got half a crown from Captain Martin (out of our pay of £2.10s. a month) every Saturday evening and the first thing we did after knock off time was to go up to Flinders Street where there was an Italian restaurant where we got soup, roast and potatoes and a pudding for 6d. The old man Antonio took the 6d, as we walked out at the door.

By early April we were loaded. By this time I had a number of friends in Melbourne, especially MacKenzie from Loch Carron and Finlayson from Skye. I met a cousin of my Father's at the MacKenzie's house. Actually his mother was a first cousin of my father's. He and his brother were missionaries in the South Sea Islands and he was on holiday in Melbourne. After the cargo of wool was loaded we were towed down to the Bay where we anchored off Williamstown for several days till we had got a crew together. I think they were a tougher crowd than the men we signed on in Glasgow. We were towed out to Port Philip's Head and then set sail for home round Cape Horn. We had a remarkably good passage and sighted no land till we got to the Lizard. We had one real gale off Cape Horn when we had to stow the mizzen lower topsail. The Captain lashed a young apprentice aged 14 to the mizzen mast. He said he was too young to go aloft on a night like that - an unusual thing for the captain. However, by next day the gale blew itself out. Whcn we got to Dungeness we were all aloft, stowing the sails for harbour stow and with the tug alongside.

I said to one of the sailors, 'You will have a beer tonight.'

'Yes,' he said, 'and I won't bother to blow the froth off.'

On the passage home there were one or two incidents. Shortly after sailing we were on salt beef again so we all had to go aft to the main hatch where the steward was handing out jugfuls of lime juice as was the custom in all sailing ships. It was compulsory in those days in order to prevent scurvy. Captain Martin was walking up and down on the poop and, I imagine, knew that the sailors he signed on in Melbourne were a tough lot. He stood and talked to the steward below him.

'Look,' he said, so that all the crew could hear him, 'at my sailors, how well they are fed. Seven courses. Burgoo (porridge), tea, biscuits, coffee, pea soup, salt-beef and lime juice.' And he kept on repeating it. 'And where would they be if they were not here? Yes,' he said, 'sleeping in the Melbourne churchyard, starving and only a newspaper to cover them on cold nights.'

One morning we were hoisting the main top gallant sail, when the Captain came on deck and he said something, nothing very derogatory, and a Welshman, a sea lawyer, answered him back. In a second the old man was down on the main deck and said that if a fight was what he wanted, he was ready. Not a cheep out of the sea lawyer so we did not see a fight between Bully Martin, over 70 years old, and a young man of under 30 years. On our arrival in London we were bundled into a coach (those that signed on in Glasgow - no motors in those days) and sent to Euston station to catch the evening train for Glasgow. The cook was lost and I was told to search for him. I found him being pushed out of a first class carriage, drunk. It was said he urinated in the carriage. I had little sympathy with him; none of the sailors liked him. He had a bad habit when we were in Melbourne of putting our tea on the stove in the galley and going ashore at 3pm and left it stewing till 6pm when he got back. The crew also complained that he was dirty and on one occasion at sea they threatened to have him out on deck and scrub him. He must, however, have been a good cook for the cabin or else the Captain would never have tolerated him. I was no sooner paid off than I was looking for another ship as I decided not to go home this time. I went aboard the *"Loch Garry"* and the mate said he would sign me on but the ship would not be sailing for another month. I then went A.B. in an Allan Liner, the *"Corinthian"*, for a voyage to Montreal. We were away for nearly a month and while in Montreal I met Ewen Kennedy and his sister who were our next door neighbours in Toscaig; otherwise the voyage was of no importance for me. By the time I got back the *"Loch Garry"* was nearly ready for sea and I signed on for the voyage. There also signed on a Malcolm MacKenzie, a young man from Kishorn and a man Matheson from Plockton. The latter was known as MacJohnacan. They had no sailing ship experience but I introduced them to the mate MacAdie from Orkney so he signed them on. Captain Horne was master, a very religious man and he used to have a service in good weather about 10.30am. The watch below did not attend service, but sometimes the apprentices went and they always were at the back and the steward was near the front. I learnt afterwards that the reason the apprentices were so keen was that they knew the chief steward left the pantry door open so one of them slipped in and got away with sugar and any other commodity ready at hand while the Captain was praying.

I heard of a very religious master of a sailing ship who insisted on both watches attending Sunday services. One day he was earnestly preaching on, 'Ye are the sheep and I am the good shepherd'. One of the tough sailors at the back shouted, 'Maa!' So the Preacher shouted back, 'Who the b..... hell said that?'

We did not make a good run south; winds were light and Captain Horne would not crack on like old bully Martin. As we sailed in August it was therefore a long run to the line. We had a few passengers (Cabin) aboard so we had aboard hens, sheep and pigs. The sailors, of course, would not get any pork when a pig was killed. An apprentice was coming down from aloft one day when all the officers and passengers were at dinner at 1pm. The officer of the watch was forward and out of sight. The dead pig was hanging on the mizzen rigging. It had to be there under the eye of the officer and Captain on the poop. The apprentice, however, had a sharp knife and he cut a quarter off on his way down. No one saw him. The apprentices could not cook in their place so they came to the forecastle with it and the watch began cooking it in a Kerosene tin. Coal was got up from the fore-peak and the cooking was done on the iron platform of the windlass. The windlass was in the centre of the forecastle so imagine the stink and the smoke coming out of the kerosene tin. It was my watch below and I fell asleep. Next day the pork was served amongst us but it was too raw for me to tackle; most of it was pushed overboard. Anyway it was a gallant attempt to improve our diet. We did not feed as well as in the *"Loch Broom"*. Nothing but the bare whack as sailors called their rations. Someone threw a few biscuits overboard one day and the Captain gave him an awful row. Old toothless sailors very often could not chew the hard biscuits so a young fellow like me with good teeth had more than I could eat of biscuits.

We had a very good passage out to Adelaide, but we did not go far south running the Easting down. Years before the *"Loch Garry"* was dismasted in a gale off the Cape of Good Hope. The three masts went overboard and it was only through superhuman efforts that the master and crew were able to cut them adrift and sail the ship under jury rig into Mauritius. At one time everyone thought the ship was gone and the Captain called the mate up to him, kissed him and said goodbye. The mate was his own son.

There is no doubt but that Captain Horne was a very fine and able seaman and was also a humanitarian and he was only carrying out orders of both the owners and the Board of Trade when he kept his crew on the rations given to him. The day after our arrival in Adelaide we Highland chaps (a good number of the crew was from the Highlands) went to church on Sunday morning and it was the same church that Captain Horne worshipped in, and that pleased him very much, I heard afterwards. We were 90 days from Glasgow to Adelaide, not a bad passage.

A young sailor from Foula Island near the Shetlands told me a story about the *"Loch Vennacher"* which he was in the voyage before. One night when approaching Kangaroo Island near Adelaide the man on the lookout came running down from the forecastle head and told either him or another man that he saw a man in his oilskins climbing up the forestay. Everyone laughed at him and said to him who would be climbing up the forestay on a beautiful night like this and anyway no one ever climbs the forestay unless perhaps the stay sail gets jammed. Next voyage the *"Loch Vennacher"* was lost with, I believe, all hands on Kangaroo Island. Weird stories like that were often debated in the forecastle.

We were not very long in Melbourne when I asked the Captain to pay me off as I was going up for my ticket (Certificate of Competency) for 2nd mate.

All the sailing ships in Melbourne at that time used to have a Boat Race on the Yarra River above the Main Bridge crossing the river. There must have been nearly a dozen sailing ships in Melbourne then and our mate was one of the keenest of the lot, so all work was stopped to clean and polish the small boat, especially the bottom. We won the race and we were cheered very much by the onlookers.

CHAPTER SEVEN

By the end of January I left the ship and went to school (navigating) and stayed with Mrs. Finlayson. Her husband was a Skyeman and he was night watchman with the Union Steamship Co. If we got only the bare rations in sailing ships, there was no scarcity of food and good cooking in the Finlaysons. In a few weeks I was lucky enough to get my ticket and now I had to look for a ship. Duncan MacRae was also looking for a ship and staying with the Finlaysons. He was from Kishorn and was then on the Coast. He and I strolled about and went down to see ships in the Dock. We always called at a fruiterers on the way back home. There was a nice looking girl serving in the shop and we named her the Peach in the Peach shop. Then one day I got a telegram from my Uncle Norman in Sydney to say that I could have a berth as 4th mate of the *"Salamis"* due the following day. I called on the Captain the next day and when he told me that I would not be in charge of a watch as 4th officer, I declined the berth there and then. The *"Salamis"* was one of the Aberdeen White Star passenger ships and their smallest. Weirs bought her in 1913 from the Aberdeen Line and I went mate of her in 1916 and was promoted to master in 1919.

Shortly afterwards I saw a big four-masted barque called the *"Glenclova"* in the dock discharging a cargo of Jarrah wood from Bunbury, Western Australia. I went aboard and saw the Captain. There was neither a mate nor 2nd mate aboard so he gave me the job as 2nd mate right away - £6.10s. a month. That was late February or early March. We discharged the cargo and then moved to Williamstown to load a cargo of wheat for home. Practically all the crew left and only the apprentices with a few men stayed in the ship. Indeed, if I remember rightly, there were no sailors in the forecastle. Loading was going on slowly and eventually we got loaded and towed into the bay. There was an old shipmaster in Williamstown who was in charge of the tallying of the wheat into the ships. The wheat was in bags so the ship was easily stowed. The Captain (his name was Bowles) asked-the old shipmaster if he would sign on as mate for the voyage home. The old man said he would for a consideration. I believe the consideration was £10, but he had no intention whatsoever of sailing in the ship and our Captain knew it. Sailing ships were not paying in those days so economies had to be made to keep them on the ocean. The Captain finally scraped a crowd together, some of them not even sailors, and one evening they all came aboard in a tug and after a couple of days we sailed about the middle of April. Immediately, the pilot came aboard he asked me if Mr. So & So was aboard. I said that I was not sure. Then he spoke to the Captain and he told me afterwards that he was enquiring for the man who signed on as mate. I suppose the shipping master told the pilot as he would be suspicious of the vessel sailing without a mate. Every ship of over 100 tons was supposed to have a master, mate and 2nd mate aboard before a certificate of clearance was given to any foreign going ship. Anyway, all the crew were aboard except the mate and it is possible the pilot had the impression that he was dead drunk. We hove up and were towed down to Port Philip's Head where we dropped the pilot and set sail with a following wind. Our voyage home began and the Captain then told me to act as mate and a young fellow from the forecastle was chosen as 2nd mate. Presumably the Captain picked him out when he signed the crew on; anyway he was a nice and capable young man.

We sailed round the south of New Zealand and the voyage was progressing fairly well with a pretty steady wind behind us moving from north west to south west and we passed well south of the Snares Stewart Island and saw no land. There was a real row on when we passed the 180° meridian. The crew generally got their rations (or whack) on Tuesdays, but it so happened that we had two Tuesdays so the sailors demanded another day's rations, but the steward refused. He would not give in, so in the end the Captain was called in and he explained to them that as they came on in Australia they had no right for a free ration. They maintained that a day was a day and that they worked it and must eat. The Captain, however, insisted that every day from now onwards till we got to the U.K. so much time was taken off the 24 hours as we were exactly 12 hours behind Greenwich time. Some way or other the crew was appeased, but they were still of the opinion that they were robbed of a day's food and I think they were right.

In spite of good fair winds we were not making a fast passage. The fact is that those heavy ships with bulging bows and sterns were poor sailors, however hard they were pushed. They were built to carry big cargoes and the *"Glenclova"* was one of the biggest carrying ships in the United Kingdom then. We passed the Bounty and other islands without seeing them. A great tragedy happened on these islands about the time we passed them. A ship (if I remember rightly called the *"Kildalton"*, if not indeed a sister ship) sailed from Sydney about the same time as we left Melbourne, loaded with wheat for the U.K. or continent. She had misty weather after passing New Zealand and did not see the sun for days and was going on dead reckoning. During the night she hit one of the Islands and was in no time a wreck. More than half the crew got ashore including the mate and 2nd mate. They lived on this small island and as the ship sank they got no rations on the island. They maintained themselves mostly on sea lions and managed to make a shelter of sorts for themselves. After the winter was over they got sufficient wood, etc, which drifted ashore to make a raft to visit another island not very far away and, as they expected, they found food on the island placed there by the New Zealand Government for shipwrecked mariners. The mate and some of the sailors died during the time they were on the small island. During the Second World War one of the MacLeay & MacIntyre cargo vessels was in Basrah and I discovered that the master of this ship was the 2nd mate who was cast away on the island. He had dinner with me and we talked of old times, but I have forgotten his tales of their hardship till they were rescued by a New Zealand survey ship exactly nine months after they were wrecked. I remember, however, how glad they were to find food and shelter on the second island and how they were quite happy and comfortable till help came their way.

When we were about half way across the Southern Pacific we got into a very heavy gale from the north and while I was trying to get forward to the break of the forecastle head and had almost got there, the ship half buried herself in a heavy sea which caught me and I floated along to the other end of the ship, actually to the break of the poop. Indeed, I was not sure whether or not I was overboard, but I remember catching some ropes and then I realised that I was still floating around the deck. I was none the worse for my ordeal. I was so seldom dry, anyway, that I don't think I changed my clothing till I went off watch.

We were plugging along not too badly when, one evening some 600 miles west of Cape Horn, the Captain told me, when I went into the cabin for tea, that never in his experience of 50 years at sea had he seen the barometer so low, just under 28 inches. We were then going along with a moderate gale of westerly wind behind us with the foresail and lower topsails on the fore main and mizzen masts and the ship not making too much bad weather of it with two men at the wheel. The wind was increasing and by the time I had my tea and went up on the poop to relieve the 2nd mate for his tea, it was a hurricane that was blowing and I had to hold on to the rigging to keep myself from being blown here and there by the wind. The Captain followed me and, as the ship was beginning to be difficult to steer, he called all hands aft except the man on the look out and another two men who were put to the wheel. By this time we could see nothing but spindrift and huge, heavy seas and it was impossible for any of us to hear one another in the gale. So there we were, all huddled on the poop and we got some ropes stretched across the deck for protection. The wind kept on increasing and nothing could be done except to try and keep the ship before the hurricane. Four men were steering her which, of course, was very difficult. At last the force of the wind sent the foresail in ribbons over the side and we wondered how the man on the lookout on the forecastle head was getting on, or did the sail take him overboard. Nothing could be done regarding him as the seas coming overboard made it impossible for anyone to go forward and look for him. Shortly after the foresail went into ribbons, the foretop sail went. This made it heavier for the men at the wheel to keep her before the heavy seas roaring in from behind us. Then the main topsail went and I remember seeing sparks of fire through the spindrift, which I suppose came from the iron chain sheets which probably broke and were banging against the yards or mast. I remember how weird it was on such a night of storm. All the foresails carried away and nothing remained of them. Steering and holding the ship before the wind was becoming impossible, especially as she started to yaw a lot and as the mizzen topsail still stood the strain, the leverage it gave to the storm kept her going from side to side. Had the foresail or fore topsail stood the strain and the mizzen topsail gone overboard, the steering would have been much easier and the chances of holding her before the wind much simpler. As things were, at about 8.30pm, she took a heavy yaw to starboard and broached to and the lee bulwark went out of sight. The mizzen topsail went in shreds and the lee side of the poop was under water. All the boats went overboard and also the standard compass. In fact we did not see them going overboard, and I suppose the thoughts of all the men on the poop were that either they themselves would be overboard soon or else the ship would capsize. She appeared to be at such an angle that it would be impossible for her to right herself. None of us except the Captain had had such an experience before. Some way or other (although he must have been getting on for 70 years old) he went down into the cabin and poured oil down the cabin watercloset and this may have helped the ship from breaking up and kept the seas from roaring aboard. I forgot to ask him how he had a large can of oil in the cabin, but a few days afterwards he told me that when he was mate of a sailing ship he had had a similar experience to ours. The Captain's wife was aboard and as the water in the cabin was getting higher and higher, she was in the end forced to hold her baby to her breast as the water was up to her waist. The other experience he had had was in the Indian Ocean in a cyclone. The ship went on her beam-end, but somehow they kept her afloat, so oil may have saved both ships and that may have been the reason he had some near at hand. Our ship was simply drifting to leeward and there is no doubt but the trickle of oil going out on the weather side kept the heavy seas from breaking aboard. Suddenly the wind about midnight began easing, but the seas remained very high. None of the crew was able to get to their quarters so we all stayed on the poop till daybreak some time about 8am, and when daylight did come, what a shambles! Some of the yards were swinging backwards and forwards and it was a miracle that none of them broke adrift and came down on deck or fell into the sea. Every sail aloft was gone and nothing remained on the yards except the ropes. As I said before, there was no sign of any of the two lifeboats or the long boat and part of the tarpaulins on the main hatch was torn, but little water got into the hold as all hatches were caulked before leaving Melbourne. The men's forecastle was gutted out. It was a large house on deck between the fore and main hatches. The galley, which was part of the house, actually the after end of it, was also gutted out and all or practically all moveable gear in it had gone overboard. The crew lost most of their clothes. The steward and the cook managed to serve some cold or tinned meat and biscuits which revived us all and there was nothing for it but to turn to and get the ship back to some sort of order and sail her again. The gale had by now settled down to a fairly strong westerly wind. After we got the yards secured and got all the ropes and halyards drifting astern on board, we went into the hold to try and shift the bags of wheat from the leeside to weather side. The whole cargo settled to leeward so that there was a large open space between the bags and the side of the ship. We dragged the bags full of wheat from the leeside to the weatherside, split them open and poured the contents down the space. At midday we came up for a meal and one watch went for a rest and by 3pm it came down to relieve the other watch for a rest. As it got dark at 5pm or before, we worked hard and were able to get the lee bulwark out of the water. The ship still had a heavy list, but the lee side of the deck was now dry. We got the ship away before dark with bare masts and were doing about 6 knots under bare poles. We were back on watch and made good progress during the night. Next morning we got busy sending our spares aloft and, although the wind and weather were cold and most of the seamen lost their clothes when the forecastle was gutted and cleaned out during the storm, by dark that day we got the foresail and topsails bent. So we made better progress. It was hard work, especially as bits of the sails and especially the leach ropes, clues, etc, got fouled of the other running gear. The following day we got the main sail and top gallant sails bent. The next day, I believe, we went below into the hold again to shift cargo as the ship had still a heavy list on her. Before dark we saw high mountains covered with snow, but we could not make out where we were, although we knew it was in the vicinity of Cape Horn, but still well to the westward of it. Water got into the chronometer in the storm and, with that and the loss of the standard compass, it was extremely difficult to fix thc position of the ship. The steering compass was hopeless and at the best of times was unreliable, but we kept a check on it through the standard compass before it went overboard. We tried to keep a course south of east and predicted by doing so that we would clear Cape Horn, by a good margin. The high mountains well on our port bow the night before gave us a clue that we were on the course.

I went on duty at 4am the next morning and, just before daybreak, the wind unfortunately shifted from west to south, with heavy snow squalls. I trimmed the yards accordingly, but now instead of a good eight knots when the wind was behind us, the old ship started "floundering" about and could not make much progress with only the fore and mainsail and six topsails on her. Anyway, although we were certainly on a lee shore, it was quite a long way off and the wind was steady on the starboard beam with heavy snow squalls. We were still a bit worried, however, so the Captain sent me aloft to see if there was any land jutting out beyond the point on the port bow.

'If,' he said, 'that is Cape Horn, we shall scramble round if the wind holds in this direction from the south and doesn't go east, but if that is not Cape Horn, then we may as well shackle the cables to the anchors and run round one of the islands near Cape Horn and endeavour to anchor the ship somewhere and get her on an even keel and get more sails bent.'

I went aloft and stood in the fore topgallant yard and could see no land south of the point on the port bow. When I reported this to the Captain, he said that we should manage round with a little to spare, but that the old ship was very sluggish.

So then I said, 'What about hoisting the lower fore-topgallant sail and that may put a little more life in her, even although she may carry too much in the squalls.'

He then said that she could carry more sail without a doubt, but all our canvas on the ship was now the worse for wear. In fact, our second best, as all the best went overboard in the gale. He gave orders to hoist the fore topgallant sail and I went below for 40 winks. When I got on deck at midday we were abreast of Cape Horn, four miles to leeward, and the Captain told me to have a look at the place through the telescope, and there I would see a smooth rock, several feet high, with the words "Tit-bits" written on it. We wondered who would have written that in such an isolated spot and we came to the conclusion a survey ship must have been there and on a fine day the sailors would have gone ashore to fix something to other or make some marks on the rocks and amused themselves by writing the above.

When we passed Cape Horn it was almost the middle of winter, the snow was down to the water's edge and no boat could land anywhere near it with a strong wind blowing on to it and very heavy waves breaking on the rocks. Cape Horn is an island so there may be smoother water on the other side of it. To us it looked the barest and barrenest place we had ever seen. At 12.30pm, we were safely round it and the order to square the yards went forward and the men in their glory to be heading north. In no time the ship was heading for the Falkland Isles with a fair steady wind.

When I went down to dinner, the Captain greeted me with these words, 'You might have been dining with the (Fuegians) Indians now or they may be making a meal of you.'

Actually the Indians down there were not cannibals, but sailors believed they were, even then. They were treacherous and went about covered with animal skins, their only covering in the winter time, but almost or altogether naked in the summer months. Anyway, there were no inhabitants in the islands around Cape Horn except perhaps fishermen in the summer months. I believe there were one or two places around there where the British Government stowed food for shipwrecked mariners.

It was refreshing to be heading north and for warmer weather, and the Captain thought of going through the Straits of Le Maire between Staten Island and the mainland as the water would be smoother and we would get a better chance to get the ship back to her old trim and condition. He had, however, second thoughts as our sailors were not suited to take any risks in narrow channels, besides, the Le Maire Straits are very treacherous with very strong currents and variable winds. The weather kept fine for several days and the wind held and we all got our sodden clothes dried out. I don't think I had any dry clothing, all were damp with the water that got into everywhere during the gale. I remember for a fact that I used to put on my long knitted stockings always wet when I put my seaboots on to go on watch. Actually very often I put them under me in bed when I went into my bunk so they were nice and warm when I got up.

I was bringing home a cockatoo and friends gave me a small kitten. The bird and the kitten were very friendly and when I left the ship I put the cat with the parrot in the cage and they were very happy in the train to Glasgow. I gave the cat to another sailor in Glasgow, but took the cockatoo home to Toscaig where he lived for years.

That reminds me that we had a ship's cat, but during the gale he must have been washed overboard for no one saw him afterwards. When the gale was at its worst, one of the apprentices swore that he saw a big ship passing us with full sails set and going at a furious rate. Someone told him next day that it was the *"Flying Dutchman"*. Whether all hands believed the story I am unable to say.

The ship had still a list on her as we could not move sufficient cargo to starboard without affecting the stowage, but the weather must have remained good for nothing much happened except the usual routine. We did not see the Falkland Islands as we passed well east of them. We, of course, bent all the sails, so we were progressing fairly well and after passing the latitude of the River Plate the wind moved over to the southwest and I remember trimming the yards and setting more sail during the night and at once we were scudding along at about 10 knots. When the 2nd mate came up at 4pm to relieve me, he said that he could not go to sleep when he went to his bunk as he was admiring my voice when I was trimming the yards. When I shouted, 'Belay there', all hands could hear me even in a gale. On the other hand when he was trimming the yards, he would have to keep on and on shouting for him to be heard on the other side of the ship and it was very annoying when one of the sailors shouted back at him, 'Did you say "belay there", sir?'

My Father, although he was a small man, had a loud, penetrating voice which carried a long way.

One evening the Captain was telling me of his experience in the ship several years back. He arrived in Melbourne and freights were low so all the sailors left the ship or were paid off and the ship was laid up. In due course freights were going up and the ship was chartered from Sydney, I believe, with grain or wool. He engaged a crowd of Riggers to sail the ship round to Sydney. He asked them to wash the deck down and they refused point blank and said that they, as Riggers, were on board to sail the ship and no other work. The weather was very hot and the Captain naturally was anxious that the seams in the deck would not open too much or otherwise his valuable cargo from Sydney would get damaged. He again appealed to them, but to no avail. That afternoon when all the sails were set, it came on to blow from the south and the ship began to heel over, but no orders came from the Captain to reduce sail. He walked up and down on the poop unconcernedly. He could see all the Riggers talking and sheltering under the forecastle head. At last a few of them came up to see him and said that they would like to see some sails coming off the ship or otherwise she would capsize.

'Too late now,' he said, 'and I am not caring whether she capsizes or not as I am nearly 70 and have not very long to live anyway. Furthermore, you would not carry out my orders to wash down the decks so I find now that you are all cowards as well as being lazy.' Luckily, shortly afterwards the wind began to decrease so all was well. Probably, the Captain, being an old sailor, had studied the winds and weather and was shrewd enough to know that the wind would not increase above a certain point. What did amuse him when he got up in the morning was seeing the Riggers busily employed washing down the decks without being told to do so. Riggers were men that sailed sailing ships from port to port for short distances and, of course, they got sailing ships ready for sea before leaving port when there were no sailors aboard.

One Captain told me another story which happened when he was master of one of the Sierra ships. There was a regular line of them from the U.K. to the East, mostly to India and they always called at St. Helena on the homeward and outward passages whenever possible. The ship he was in (I believe it was called the *"Sierra Nevada"*) was getting under way and was on the correct tack to get out of the harbour, when, just then, a big sailing man of war with the Admiral aboard hove up her anchor and some way or other fouled his ship. Angry words passed between the Captains and the Admiral shouted to him to get out of his way, to which he replied that if the Admiral knew his business he would have handled his ship in a more seamanship manner.

'I believe,' he said to me, 'that I was the only master in the merchant service that ever told an Admiral to go to hell.'

We were soon in the south-east trade winds and sighted St. Paul's Rocks. The Captain thought it would be possible to correct his chronometer as we knew it was wrong. Sights were taken, but the distance between us and St. Paul's Rocks could not possibly be correctly estimated, nor could we get bearings to ascertain the distance.

We were not long in the Doldrums, when we got the northeast trades. After losing the northeast trades we went due north instead of steering a direct course to Queenstown or Falmouth, passing fairly close to the Azores Islands, commonly known to sailors as the Western Isles. Our reason for steering due north was a common sense one as our chronometer was miles out and our compass gyrated like a spinning top. We were almost in mid Atlantic before we reached latitude 49 north and then we got on the latitude of the Lizard and steered due east. The Captain told us two mates to keep the Pole Star on the port beam and we should not go far wrong. Luckily we had a fair wind, not once did the wind go against us. When we got into the "chops" of the channel, it was misty and visibility very poor and we were afraid we would pass Falmouth and would have a job to get back. We hove the deep sea lead and found sand and shells. We shackled the cables to the anchors and everything was ready for an emergency. We cautiously groped our way eastwards with a slight southerly wind, hoping we were still west of Falmouth. I went below at 8pm; it was my watch below, but I did not take my clothes off as I was thinking I might be called any minute to wear or tack ship. Sure enough, about 11pm, I heard a terrible din going on on deck and someone shouting, 'All hands on deck.' I was not long getting on to the poop and there was the Captain directing operations and giving orders to wear ship. Indeed, the ship was obeying the helm already and some of the yards were smartly coming round for the port tack. I asked the Captain the cause of the commotion and he said,

'Look astern and there you will see St. Mary's light on the Scilly Isles. Luckily,' he said, 'I saw it in the starboard bow through the mist and if I had not been quick enough to up helm, we would have been now piled up on the Island.'

We were now in a quandary and on the port tack on the way to Ireland. The wind was still in the south and to get round the Scilly

Isles with the wind becoming lighter and it still misty was a doubtful problem. Anyway, we now knew we were north and west of the Scilly Isles which was a comfort, even if we were a bit lost. When the morning arrived it cleared up a bit, as old sailors used to say, 'The sun swallowed the mist'. No land, however, was in sight and we were still moving slowly westwards and thought now of directing our course to Queenstown. Our orders were Queenstown or Falmouth. At about 10am we got sights using the chronometer and at noon we got the latitude. The Captain then had the chart to fix our position and to our consternation our position at noon was in a green field in Devon! We then realised how hopeless was the chronometer and that it must be at least 60 miles out as, of course, we were still afloat northwest of the Scillies. As the wind was steady from the south, there was nothing for it but to steer a course for Queenstown, very difficult indeed with the ship in a green field and the only compass very, very erratic. A course was steered for Queenstown with a leading wind and all sails were set and we were bowling along at nearly 10 knots hoping the wind would hold and we would be in Queenstown in the morning. All was going according to plan and I took the Royals in at about midnight as I thought that there was no point in carrying too much sail as the wind was increasing and we were steering more or less in a lee shore.

During my watch below (again I did not take my clothes off), I heard a terrible din on deck and somebody shouting to wake up the watch below and all hands on deck. A flashing light was sighted and it did not correspond with the Old Head Kinsale Lighthouse. There was nothing to do but to get away from the land and wear ship as soon as possible. I spoke to the Captain on the poop and he certainly knew it was not the Old Head of Kinsale, which was the light we expected to pick up. So we decided to tack ship and have all hands on deck. When I got forward some of my watch were crawling out and others not yet ready so I told them to get a move on as we might be on the rocks any minute.

I heard someone saying, 'To hell with it, anyway. I am fed up and it is just as well some of us were drowned.'

It was very dark at the time and, of course, the sailors were worn out, but I don't think they would have been hungry. The cook made fresh bread every day, but we were a bit short of meat as some of the meat casks stored on deck or above the galley or in front went overboard in the gale. We got the ship down to topsails and decided to wait till daylight before making a move. We were, however, more or less certain that the light we saw was Minehead, some 50 miles north of the Old Head Kinsale. If so, with the wind going more to the west, we could not expect to beat up against the wind to get into Queenstown that day. The morning brought the sun out, but it was still misty and we could not see the land. A big ship passed close to us and at once we decided to ask her for our position. Before we got our flags out of their lockers and hoisted for information about our position, the Cunarder S/S *"Etruria"* was going out of sight. She was probably doing over 20 knots so was soon lost in the mist. Anyway luck came our way. The weather cleared and the wind came out fresh from the southwest and there was Minehead Lighthouse some five or six miles on our starboard.

I went to breakfast and the first words the Captain said to me were, 'It is a pity we lost all our boats, otherwise I would go closer to the land and send you ashore for potatoes (we had, of course, had no potatoes for four months) for they must be very plentiful in those beautiful fields near the lighthouse.'

After examining the land and the lighthouse and the white and black stripes around it we were certain of our position. The wind was now fresh from the southwest so it was decided that it was much easier to get to Falmouth with a fair wind than trying to beat up to Queenstown, so it was a case of up helm again and set a course for the Scilly Isles. This time we gave them a wide berth and when we got on to our course we were more certain of the compass deviation. Recognising our position and the lay of the land we obtained something that gave us confidence and we knew that if the wind held and no more fog or mist arose we would round the Scilly Isles with a good margin of safety. What we lacked before this was to get a position of the ship with any accuracy. Next morning, sure enough, there were the Scilly Isles on our port. We made good progress over from Ireland with a fresh wind and all sails set. We rejoiced to see the Islands and when we got round and squared the yards for Falmouth, the breeze kept up and we picked up a tug around the Lizard and were anchored in Falmouth before dark. Indeed, I think we were anchored early in the afternoon. Boats were alongside with all sorts of good things with everything from a needle to an anchor; that is, of course, a sailor's exaggeration, but all seafaring people used this term when talking about big stores ashore. In our case most of the sailors went for fruit and cakes and I have not the slightest doubt but beer was in some of the boats although this was not allowed. I sent a telegram home that we arrived safely and I was hoping to get home soon.

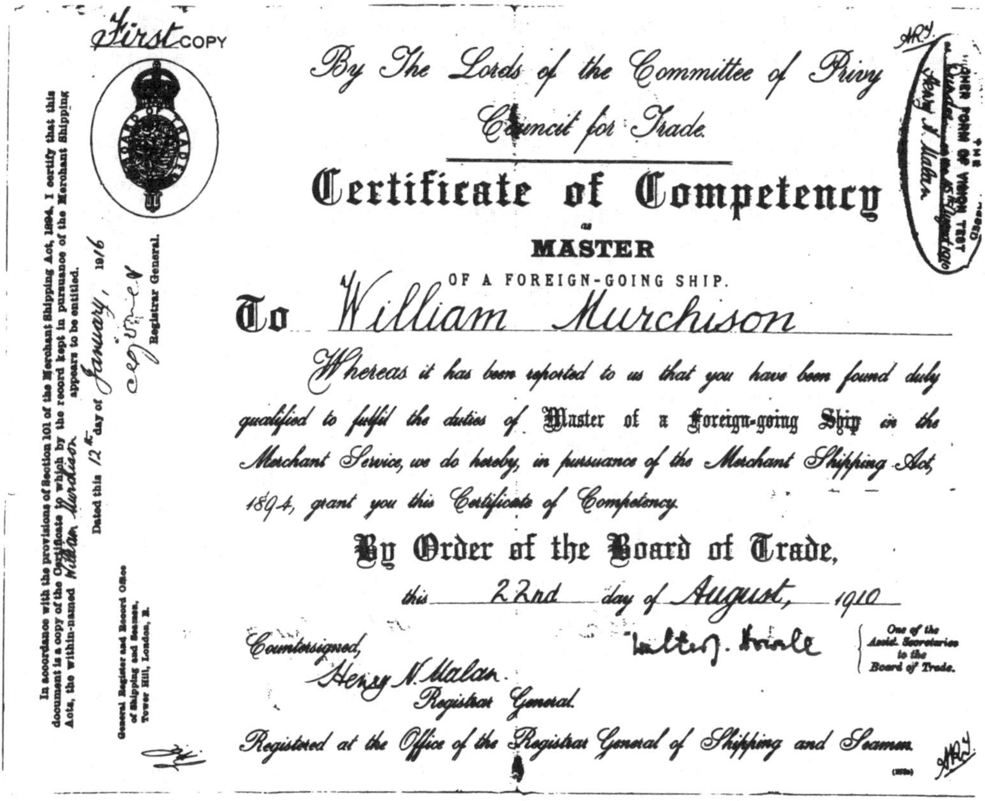

First COPY

In accordance with the provisions of Section 101 of the Merchant Shipping Act, 1894, I certify that this document is a copy of the Certificate to which by the record kept in pursuance of the Merchant Shipping Acts, the within-named William Murchison appears to be entitled.

Dated this 12th day of January, 1916

Registrar General.

General Register and Record Office of Shipping and Seamen, Tower Hill, London, E.

By The Lords of the Committee of Privy Council for Trade.

Certificate of Competency

as

MASTER

OF A FOREIGN-GOING SHIP.

To William Murchison

Whereas it has been reported to us that you have been found duly qualified to fulfil the duties of Master of a Foreign-going Ship in the Merchant Service, we do hereby, in pursuance of the Merchant Shipping Act, 1894, grant you this Certificate of Competency.

By Order of the Board of Trade,

this 22nd day of August, 1910

Countersigned, Henry N. Malan. Registrar General.

Walter J. Howell — One of the Assist. Secretaries to the Board of Trade.

Registered at the Office of the Registrar General of Shipping and Seamen.

We were several days at Falmouth before getting orders to go to Cardiff for discharging the cargo. The next day an ocean tug came alongside and we sailed more or less at once. When we got round the Lizard and were well on our way to Lands End, the tow rope parted and there we were on our own again. The wind was still from the south west with quite a choppy sea and ground swell coming in from the Atlantic. Anyway, we had not drifted much before the tug was almost alongside of us and shouting to give them a line to get another tow rope. This was done so, again, we were on the move. Next day we were in Cardiff Roads and were ordered into dock at once. I was wondering how to dress going into dock as there was no uniform in those days. In the end I put on my best blue suit and a bowler hat, so I quite imagined myself as somebody on the forecastle head with a bowler hat. How odd it would look today. The Captain of sailing ships, especially the old ones, used to wear frock coats and tall hats, much taller than the bowler. Old Bully Martin in the *"Loch Broom"* never went ashore without his frock coat and top-gallant hat, as the old sailors named the tall hats.

Thus, indeed, ended a very hazardous voyage and looking back on it, I realise how dangerous was the life of sailing ship men and how lightly they took their calling. There was so much work to be done that one never thought of the perils. That morning we were closing in on Cape Horn, I remember vividly looking over the port side of the ship before daylight and, after the wind changed to the south, imagining the ship was sinking for there was very little freeboard when the ship listed over. So sure was I that she was leaking that I told the carpenter to sound the ship before the usual time. He reported no water, but it shows how people's imaginations can deceive them, especially on a very dark night.

I remember a story the Captain of a ship told me once. He was mate of his father's Cornish schooner and on their way from Seville with oranges to the U.K. One morning near Cape St. Vincent, Spain, they sighted a schooner fully laden with salt but behaving in a queer manner. He boarded her and found no one aboard, so he came back and told the Captain, his Father.

'Go back aboard,' he said, 'and follow me to Gibraltar as the wind is favourable.'

Next day he sailed her into the harbour and his Father went ashore to report to the British Consul. Who were at the Consulate, but the Captain and crew, making a statement that their schooner was lost and sunk, they swore, a couple of nights before. What really happened was this: they were sailing as usual in a heavy swell and before going off watch the mate sounded the ship. He looked at his sounding iron stick and the line and it was wet half way up. He dried it and, sure enough, it gave the same result. He reported to the Captain and the Captain got the same result when he tried. Someone then said the ship was sinking and some looked over the side and confirmed on a dark, inky night that the ship was sinking, so all hands took to the boats and left the schooner. All that really happened was that with the movement of the ship some vapour of the salt cargo moved up the sounding pipe and caused the inside of it to be wet; the men's imagination in the darkness did the rest, and one can only imagine the remarks of the crew when they saw their ship at anchor.

To get back to my ship, we got paid off the next day and I took the evening train to Glasgow. Before going home I decided to look for another ship, so went to the Baron Steamers, H. Hogarth & Sons' office in spite of my experience in the *"Baron Huntly"* as a seaman. They offered me a job as 3rd mate in the *"Baron Cawdor"* due home in three weeks' time. I packed my bag for Applecross as I had not been home for about two years. I forgot to mention that our trip in the *"Glenclova"* took 123 days, not too bad for a ship of her type and the fact that we lost several days moving about in the Irish Sea. I did not have much money as I took an advance of my pay in Melbourne before sailing to pay Mrs. Finlayson for lodging for most of my time ashore and waiting for a ship. I had been six months in the *"Glenclova"* at £6.10s. a month with no extra pay for acting mate. Anyway, I arrived home with about £20 which was a considerable amount in those days. I gave most of it to my mother as a job was promised me in three weeks. I really should have stayed longer at home, but was anxious to get the other six months of my time in. Three weeks holiday after practically two years hard work would not suit people today, and there were no holidays with pay then. However, I enjoyed the holiday and my brother Roderick was at home. Indeed he met me with a sailing fishing boat at Kyle of Lochalsh. The fishing boats of those days were called skiffs. When we left the pier at Kyle of Lochalsh, I took the helm but Roderick said I luffed her up too much so took the helm himself. Perhaps I was out of tune with the small sailing boat. This was in August 1907.

CHAPTER EIGHT

The three weeks were not long in passing, so I had to leave to join the *"Baron Cawdor"* as 3rd mate at Hull. In a way I was glad to be back in steam with its ease and comfort. Little to do but keep watch while at sea. In another way I was a bit sorry for engaging myself to a life on a steamer and thought then that I should have another year in a sailing ship as 2nd mate or mate. In those days British sailing ships were being sold to foreigners and none was being built and it was common knowledge that there was no future for them. Here I was now a watch keeping 3rd mate with £6 a month. It was a great advantage to have three mates. The watch and watch 4 hours each was abolished and in its place one was on duty 8 hours in the 24. There were still lots of steam ships running with only two mates in the year 1907.

I signed on in Hull and in a day or two we were on our way to Barry Dock where we were to bunker for the voyage. Coal was cheap in those days and bunkers could be put on board for 12/- a ton and Welsh coal was the best steaming coal. We left Barry Dock early in October for Newport, U.S.A., where we were to load a full cargo of coal for Honolulu to bunker the American fleet on their way on a round the world voyage via Australia. A large number of tramp steamers followed us on the same mission. This was an entirely out of the way voyage for the Baron boats. The normal charters were coal to some Eastern ports like Aden or Perim, then salt to India. The Captain of the *"Baron Cawdor"* was a Nova Scotian, or Blue Noses, as they were termed in those days. Nothing eventful happened across the Atlantic or till we were approaching the Magellan Straits in the middle on summer. We only called at St. Lucia for bunkers and one Indian sailor fell overboard, but we rescued him. There was no Panama Canal then. The Straits of Magellan were certainly tricky navigation and the Captain was very nervous of this part of the world where he had never been before. There were only a few hours of darkness but nevertheless it was decided to anchor for the night and get away early next morning. Where we were anchored a native canoe came alongside with men and women in it, all clad in skins and very little of them. We were soon past Cape Pilar and into the Pacific. We got into a gale with very heavy westerly waves and all the crew were remarking on them. As I was further south earlier in the year, actually six months before I thought very little about them and here we were with a screw in our stern which would push us any way we wanted to go. It was child's play compared to handling frozen canvas sails. It was a very long journey to go right up the Pacific, but at last we sighted the highest peak in Honolulu over a hundred miles away and next morning we were in our berth at the Admiralty pier. The man in charge refused to take the Bill of Lading quantity less 2½% which was a customary usage at that period for coal cargoes and, as the coal was automatically weighed whilst loading it and the draught of the ship confirmed the weight more or less, it was a senseless request to have it weighed and delay the discharging and the ship. Orders were orders, however, so it was all weighed. Now the day arrived when there was a huge heap on the wharf and the ship was empty, but would have to wait till all the coal was weighed. The captain had a telegram confirming that the ship was chartered to carry a cargo of wheat from Portland, Oregon, to the Mediterranean or U.K. or continent and that utmost dispatch be given to the ship as she must be at the loading berth on a given date. Now the old Captain was in a quandary as his ship was empty, but immobilised through the weighing. However, he took the bull by the horns and went straight to the man in charge and asked him what it was worth to let the ship away.

'I guess, Captain, it will cost you 500 dollars.' The old Captain nearly fainted for out East a little settlement like that would cost a few rupees and he knew very well his owners in Glasgow would take a poor view of it and that he would be lucky if he did not get the sack for squandering their money. He was, however, between the devil and the blue sea but the devil won, for if he lost the charter God alone knows what might happen. We sailed the next morning after writing carefully with all sorts of explanations to his owners. But the whole matter worried him and it came on to blow the evening before we were due to arrive at Portland, Oregon, which put the ship on a lee shore. He must have thought that I listened to him more sympathetically than the other officers for he often came up on the Bridge before going to bed and talked for a while and this evening he was worried and talked about a lee shore.

'Why worry?' I said. So I told him about my last Captain off Cape Horn and that he did not worry himself a bit. 'And here you are with a propeller to move the ship around and you have far less cause to worry, and you worry.'

The next day the pilot came aboard at noon and when the Captain and the other officers went down for lunch, or dinner as we normally called it, the pilot asked me if I came from the Highlands and when I said I did, he said that his great-grandfather MacDonald came from the Island of Barra. But still I was surprised to hear him speaking Gaelic to me. He explained, however, that he was born in Nova Scotia and Gaelic was his first language like myself. We got alongside the loading berth at about 6pm and when we were moored the mate and 2nd mate went in for tea and I was on duty on deck. When they finished I went into the saloon for tea and the Captain came in immediately afterwards as he was delayed talking to the ships' agents. He had several letters in his hand and started reading one of them and by the time he had only read a few lines, he was reading loudly to himself and now and again he would stop. The owners were giving him hell for giving so much money away in Honolulu and they ended the letter by asking him if he thought they were a philanthropic society. By this time he was very angry and speaking to himself and took no notice of me. He then picked up his wife's letter who lived in Liverpool with three daughters. When he opened it he said in a loud voice, 'My dear Harry, Mary got the flu, Jeanie got the measles, the Baby has got the croup and I am not feeling well myself.'

Then he picked all the letters up, flung then to the other end of the table and said, 'To Hell with them all. Let us have our tea.'

Hell really was not the word he used. A much more bitter and vulgar one. If, of course, he had read his wife' s letter first, he would have had a more peaceful mind.

We were loaded in no time and sailed, and had to go as far north as Nanaimo in Vancouver Island to get our bunkers. We got into a very bad gale just south of the Aleutian Islands, hove to and smashed in our boats. When we crossed the 180° meridian on a

Thursday night we told the Lascar crew the next day to knock off work at midday as this was Saturday.

'No, sahib,' the Serang said. 'It is Friday.'

There was no use arguing with him. Shortly afterwards the whole crew came along to the Bridge Deck to say that they did not understand the reasons for missing a day, but would the Captain tell them where Mecca was so that they could face towards it in their evening prayers.

We called at Japan for more bunkers and eventually we arrived in Antwerp to discharge our cargo. As usual I took boat and train to Glasgow and, as I had my time in with a little to spare, I went to school there and within a couple of weeks I sat the 1st mate's examination and got through. There were new regulations for eye testing and the examiner congratulated me about my good eyesight as I made no mistake whichever eye I used. After a week or so I was away to sea again, this time in the *"Baron Lovat"* as 2nd mate. I wasn't keen on the job as the vessel only carried two mates but she only traded to and from the Mediterranean ports. She was just bought by the firm and was pretty old. She had a whale back forecastle head so my only vivid recollection of this ship was once in a dense fog. We were on our way from Algiers to Huelva and the fog was very thick east of Gibraltar, but we nosed our way through it expecting to hear the Gun on the Point any minute after 4pm, at last we heard it before dark, but it was not very clear and not at all regular. Anyway, it was decided that it was the Gun fog signal sure enough so course was altered to pass a few miles off it in a NNW direction. Finally at about 8pm the fog cleared and we were heading straight for the land with Gibraltar light on our port bow instead of our starboard bow and far off our dead reckoning position. It would have been impossible to hear the Gun fog signal from the spot the ship was in. Now we wondered what made the noise we had heard about 2 or 3 hours before, but there was no explanation till one night we heard it again on a clear night. What apparently caused the noise of the "gun" we heard was the man on the lookout. When he was walking up and down on the small space allowed on the whale back forecastle head, he stood on a thin iron plate which yielded to his heavy feet but jumped back with a bang when he got off it. This was remedied when we got to Glasgow but the ship might have gone ashore through a fault nobody could explain and but for a very strong easterly current going through Gibraltar Channel which took at least two knots off our estimated speed, it is possible we might have hit rocks before sighting land in such a dense fog. Equipment for navigation in those days was very poor indeed and a large number of masters had to supply their own charts. There is a story about the Captain of a sailing ship in the Islands of Polynesia in the Pacific who was navigating his ship to get to a certain island with only his own blue back chart (with only a very small scale) taking in the whole Pacific. He was tacking his ship for a fortnight to get round an island. This island turned out in the end to be a fly spot.

These short voyages I did not like, although I was not losing time for master as we were not paid off on our arrival back. What really happened, we were paid off and on the same hour. I made several voyages to the Mediterranean, coal out and either copper or iron ore home. One voyage we loaded esparto grass for Granton. By November I left the old ship and was promised a ship, the *"Baron Fairlie"* homeward from Calcutta. I had a holiday at home and joined the *"Baron Fairlie"* in Dundee in the first days of January 1909 as 2nd mate. With a Lascar crew, we went to Barry to load coal for Aden, then to Calcutta with salt. This turned out to be a long voyage. We made several voyages from Calcutta to various ports on the Indian Coast, once as far as Karachi, then we went light from Nizampatnam after discharging coal, to Saigon where we loaded a cargo of rice for Reunion. From there light to Java where we loaded a cargo of sugar in bags in Surabaya and Tegal for Suez. The Captain, the chief mate and the engineers were not getting on very well and there were complaints about the food. One Thursday on the Java Coast there were no bacon and eggs for breakfast. The engineers said no bacon and eggs for breakfast, no steam and we will stop the ship. Some way or other the Indian steward got a few eggs together so all was well. It amazes me, even to this day, how short-sighted some British shipowners were in not supplying their ships with plenty of good food. In 1910 in Java one could buy eggs at about a 1d. a dozen and it was the custom in those early days for all the officers and engineers to have two eggs and a good share of bacon on Thursday and Sunday mornings. Why that was a custom even in the meanest tramps I cannot say, but there was no excuse for not having them, especially out east where everything was so cheap, not only food, but clothes. I myself bought six drill white cotton suits while I was in this ship for 18 rupees, equivalent to £1.4s. made to order. When a Lascar crew was aboard, the Chief Cook was normally a Mohammedan and they were not keen on frying bacon. The Captain's wife was aboard and when I was on duty (on watch) at sea between noon and 4pm she often talked to me. The Bridge was just a continuation of the Bridge deck so she normally sat there. She belonged to the East Coast of Scotland and told me one day that all her neighbours in her village were very jealous of her when her husband went off to sea. In other words she got rid of him.

To get back to Dundee, I missed a story about an incident that happened while we were discharging the cargo. The 4th Engineer was an Anglo Indian who had joined the ship and was born and brought up in Calcutta. He and I went up town one day and while we were gazing into the shop windows it began to snow.

He kept on brushing the flakes of snow off his coat but at last he said to me, 'Who is throwing these flakes down on us from the top windows?'

He had never seen snow in his life. He was feeling the cold very much so the 3rd Engineer told him to put a brick in the boiler furnace to heat it up, then put it at the end of the bed. This he did and nearly put the ship on fire as his bedclothes caught fire.

In due course we arrived at Suez. The stevedoring gangs were the worst I ever saw. They kept on tearing the bags of sugar as they were being hove out of the hold. The mate could not stand it any longer so he swore and cursed at the stevedore and his gangs right in front of the door of the Saloon. The Captain came rushing out of the saloon.

"Mr. Blair,' he said, 'my wife is in the saloon, so you must stop that foul language.'

'To hell with your bloody wife,' said the mate, who was now exasperated. 'Just you look at these bags of sugar.'

We were not long in Suez discharging our cargo and from there were ordered to load at Aden a full cargo of salt for Calcutta where we discharged the crew and got a new one. While we were discharging the salt there was a coal strike in Australia and all coal mines were left idle. The Australian Government got busy and started chartering ships and buying coal wherever they could obtain it. A large number of ships were chartered in the U.K. to take coal out, and from Calcutta a large number of tramp steamers were chartered and obtained good freights. We were soon on our way with a cargo of coal for Sydney for orders. When we got to Sydney Heads we got orders to go to Melbourne and there we discharged our cargo and loaded a cargo of wheat for U.K. or continent. As the coal was urgently required we got a double quick dispatch and we were soon on our way home. We had not enough bunkers to take us to Durban so we had to call at Bunbury, Western Australia, to get bunkers there. Coal was in such a demand, however, and so many ships waiting there for it that our turn to get away appeared far into the future. Furthermore, the coal obtainable there was of a very poor quality. There we lay at anchor for weeks and nothing much to do but fishing; week after week passed, but at last after a six weeks' stay we got our orders to move to the coal loading berth and were away the next day.

The coal we had got was indeed of a very poor quality and we made very slow progress. I was on the 12 midnight watch to 4am and Halley's Comet was sweeping across the Southern Hemisphere in the southern latitudes. It was a great sight and as the nights were mostly clear, it was in sight my whole watch. The old sailors took a gloomy view of the Comet for they were sure some disaster would come along, but their real beliefs were that a great man or woman would be sure to die whilst it was roaming about the skies.

We called at Mauritius for bunkers as our bunkers were going down at an alarming rate. There was no wireless in tramp steamers in those days, but everything in the world was going along normally, when we got to Mauritius in spite of the comet. We got away the same day and were now on our way to Durban. The comet pushed its nose above the horizon on my watch and serenely went its way to the westward. The Chief Engineer and, I believe, the Captain were still looking for something to happen and they said, just you wait! On our arrival in Durban the first news the pilot told us was that King Edward had died and the Chief said, I told you so.

Our trip home was uneventful and even the passage round the Cape of Good Hope was smooth, not very usual for the beginning of winter down there. We put into Cape Town for more bunkers and got orders there to proceed to Lisbon to discharge our cargo there. We made slow progress as the bottom of the ship was full of barnacles, especially from our long wait at Bunbury. Nothing of importance happened at Lisbon. The receivers of the cargo accused the mate of bleeding some bags to fill others so as not to be short of the number of tags on the Bill of Lading. The mate, I know, took the precaution of receiving empty bags from the shippers as experience taught him that all receivers of cargoes "cooked" the tallies if it was possible to do so. The ship then paid for a shortage which was in reality not there. The owners naturally "slated" the Captain and mate and they got the blame for the shortage through taking insufficient interest in the ship and her owners. In a place like Lisbon the tallyman could easily be bribed. In the end, of course, the Mutual Insurance kept up by shipowners paid for the shortage. Our shortage of bags could not be very serious for we heard nothing about it beyond the quarrel in Lisbon.

We loaded part cargo in Lisbon for Glasgow and there we were all paid off. Through the quarrel about the stopping of the ship, or rather the threatened one between the engineers and the Captain over the bacon and eggs episode, I was called in to the office as, presumably, the Captain thought I would be a reliable witness, but as I thought the matter should never have happened at sea, when I was questioned by the owners, I was very noncommittal. Had all the officers and engineers been brought up on a Highland croft, they would certainly not have had such fancy ideas about food. Indeed ham and eggs were never dished out, except when men and women were extremely hard worked in spring-time. It was then a luxury for about a month only, if it could be afforded, although there were always eggs on the croft.

This was in June 1910 and I had to go to school to go up for my master's certificate. I was so confident that I knew all the work that I decided to go before the examiner in 10 days. A foolish thing to do really. I should have stayed in school for at least three weeks. The exams lasted for about three or four days but on the last day the examiner left us and went to see the first flying machines that ever came to Scotland - on exhibition only. When he got back he seemed out of sorts, perhaps something angered him and when I went before him he questioned me on ships' business. He did not think I had sufficient knowledge of it and asked me to come before him next week and study the business meantime. I was naturally very disappointed. In those days if one made one mistake in any sum or in seamanship one was failed and had to do the whole lot again the following week and be correct in every item. A barbarous system. The examiner was notorious for slating candidates and would say anything to them whether it flustered them or not. I suppose he took the view that sailors should not have nerves.

On one occasion he was examining a man in seamanship who kept on saying, 'I would take my vessel this way or that way,' and kept on referring to his vessel till at last the examiner roared back at him and said, 'Dash it man, a pisspot is a vessel.'

The young man should have said a ship.

Another time he was examining a candidate in colours who appeared to know more about colours than he did, so when all the colours (skeins of wool) were on the table, he was picking them up and kept on saying this is mauve, brown, heliotrope, etc etc etc.

At last the examiner roared at him, 'Damn it,' he said, 'is your girl a dressmaker?'

All the candidates had to do was pick out the blues, reds and greens and he was not interested in other colours. I, of course, was not very keen on studying further so I went for a long weekend to Dundee to see Mr. and Mrs. Blair. Mr. Blair was mate of my last ship. I told him my story and he said, 'Why not try your luck in Dundee and put in your papers for sitting the examination next week here?'

I did so and within a week I was the proud possessor of a master mariner's certificate and could command any kind of ship from a rowing boat to a full rigged ship or a liner. After a few days I was on my way home and meant to have a long holiday after a voyage of 18 months. I called at Oban to see Uncle William on the way home. My brother John was steward in a yacht which called regularly at Oban. John looked well in his brass buttons and he was proud of the fact that he heard two girls who had just passed him on the street saying to each other, 'What a lovely, beautiful boy!' He was a nice looking man with fair hair.

I must have stayed a good while at home this time, probably about two months. I know it was the longest holiday I had had for many a year and no doubt I would have been of good use in the croft, scything hay and corn and bringing it to the barn. Everything had to be carried on one's back. Things were different too as far as I was concerned for there were no holidays with pay in those days so one had to save in order to have any sort of holiday.

I was offered and accepted a 2nd mate's berth in the *"Baron Ogilvy"* and I was away again in Liverpool where she was discharging rice from Burma. The Captain of this ship was a bit old-fashioned, especially in navigation. My cousin, Finlay MacDonald, had sailed with him as mate a good number of years before. He told me a story about him. On their arrival in Calcutta on one voyage, his wife was with him and he told the mate and 2nd mate in a very gleeful manner that his wife was expecting a baby and they were both praying it would be a boy. No sooner was the ship in dock in Calcutta than a few prophets were aboard saying they could tell you the future for years to come. The mates were not interested in their future, but they told one of them, a venerable old man with a flowing white beard, to go into the saloon and see the Captain and his wife and tell them a son was going to be born to them soon. Both the Captain and the wife were delighted to get their fortunes read and paid the old soothsayer more than the usual tip. Sure enough, a son was born a couple of months after the ship got home.

To get back to my own affairs, we sailed from Liverpool to Barry Dock and loaded coal for Rio de Janeiro and after discharging there we went light to New York and loaded case oil for Shanghai. There used to be in those days a great seal of chartering tramp steamers with case oil (that was a wooden case with two four gallon paraffin tins inside) to China and Japan. The stevedores in New York were very efficient in loading case oil and we were not very long there. One of the Indian crew took a grudge against the steward and the ship in general and went ashore and got an American lawyer to attach the ship. I was amazed when this young lawyer came aboard and attached a document to the main mast stating the Indian's many grievances and that the ship was under arrest until all these grievances were settled. The Captain was furious when he got aboard and in no time was at the lawyer's office threatening him, unless he apologised. Things were very quickly settled and the Serang (Bosun) of the crew had the young seaman on the mat and told him what he thought of him.

Captain Bridger of the *"Baron Ogilvy"* had been for a long time with the company. I am not sure, but I think he joined them as an apprentice. Crossing the Atlantic once in a light ship, a steamer without a deep tank water ballast, one of the sailors who was chipping rust in the hold complained of a sore finger and when he was taken before the Captain his whole hand was swollen and his finger black and a lump in his armpit. The Captain at once said that there was no cure but one and that was to take his finger off. It was blowing a gale at the time and the ship could not make any headway so consequently she lay wallowing in a beam sea and rolling from gunwale to gunwale, as old sailors used to describe heavy rolling. The sailor, however, was laid out on the saloon table with the Serang and six sailors holding him down. The Captain was a very particular man and he was determined to make a grand job of it. He cut it in a leisurely fashion below the knuckle so that he could have a good lump of skin to fold back over the stump. The sailor was howling as nothing was given him or any anaesthetics supplied to ease the pain. The more the sailor shouted, the more the Serang shouted to shut up, all in Hindustani. At last the Captain snapped the finger off and folded the skin carefully over the stump. The sailor rested for a day or two and was back at work before the ship's arrival at Philadelphia. The doctor of the Harbour Authorities made his usual routine round after the ship's arrival in dock so the sailor was taken to the doctor for an examination. He looked at the finger and the sailor for a while and then turned to the Captain and said, 'Well Captain, you saved his life and made an excellent job, but for your information, we doctors would never be so particular as you have been, so congratulations.'

After loading our case oil, we anchored off the Statue of Liberty to await our bunkers and while there a gale sprang up during the night. Just shortly before the gale came along a barge full of coal, deeply laden, was placed alongside of us. During the night, this barge was bumping heavily against the ship and when daylight arrived the man in charge of it discovered quite a lot of water in the hold and then realised his barge was leaking, and I never saw a man pick up his belongings so quickly before climbing a rope to safety on our ship. His barge sank very quickly, he was an Italian and had little English. Another barge load of coal came alongside and in the afternoon we sailed for Shanghai.

We had a red headed young man as 3rd mate from Hull. He was appointed while we were discharging cargo in Hull and said to me that when he saw the ship the first time with *"Ardrossan"* on her stern, he thought the ship was a foreigner. The Chief Engineer was within hearing of us and as he was an Ardrossan man, he was furious that any man in the British Isles should make such a statement.

'Young man,' he said, 'go back to school and learn geography.'

He was a nice young man and he told me that for a while he was very much in love with a parson's daughter, but one day the parson chased him with a stick though he was nimble enough to jump over the garden wall before a blow from the stick got him. The stick, however, got broken on the stone wall. Needless to say, that was the end of the romance. He stuttered and if he got a bit excited he stuttered more and more. Captain Bridger, when he was working out the ship's position at noon, had the 2nd mate beside him. Our 3rd mate was promoted to 2nd mate as the 2nd mate had to go to hospital in New York. Anyway, the Captain's habit was to ask the 2nd mate every line of figures as he completed them to see if both agreed.

The conversation was like this: the Captain would shout, 'What is your Polar distance?'

The 2nd mate would say, '23°...' stutter, stutter, stutter.

The Captain, who was very short-tempered, would shout, 'Spit it out, man, spit it out, man!'

The 2nd mate would say, 'Sir, 23° 14'...' more stutter.

And then the Captain would shout, 'Sing it, man!'

I would have finished my sums and have the ship's position while listening to all this in the chartroom and very much amused. Anyway, the ship got to Algiers without a fault in our navigation and we bunkered there and got a new 2nd mate.

I have missed the story of something which occurred while we were in Rio de Janeiro. A revolution was on between the Navy and the Army and the Army kept on trying to hit a small torpedo boat from a hill above the town. Somehow or other they always missed her when she was out in the bay. When things became too hot for her, she made a beeline for the lee side of our ship and was, of course, very well protected and it became impossible for the Army to fire on her for if they did the British Navy would be after them for damaging a British ship. The torpedo boat was air conditioned right through and the officers had lovely quarters. Air conditioning is common today, but in those days it was unheard of.

I am not sure if it was on this voyage out East, and when crossing the Indian Ocean, that something happened which I must relate. The Chief Engineer was standing by to get into the lavatory but the place was occupied. Minutes passed and then half an hour and no sign of the occupant coming out. At last, feeling curious, he looked in through the port hole and saw the 4th Engineer studying an atlas.

So he shouted to him and said, 'Study your atlas in your room.'

When the 4th Engineer got out, he said, 'I am sorry, Chief, but I am awfully constipated and I was studying the atlas really as I have calculated that there is about a 1,000 miles between my motions, reckoning that the ship makes 250 miles per 24 hours.'

It seems to me now ridiculous of shipowners in those days to confine the officers and crew into such a small space. There was ample room on the bridge deck of all tramp steamers to have large airy rooms for the mates and engineers and have at least two lavatories and bathrooms. No money was saved through the little boxes of rooms and very often two in a room, and here was a ship with only one lavatory for the officers and engineers and fours apprentices, a total of eleven men, on a deck below the bridge deck, which was almost impossible to reach in bad weather and very often difficult to use as the ship pitched and rolled.

In due course we arrived in Colombo where we bunkered and got a new crew. The new crew came down from Calcutta and went on duty immediately they came on board. Some of the apples we bought in New York were still on board and the steward told the cook to have apple pudding for dinner at 1pm. It was the Captain's favourite pudding, but God help the poor cook if it was stodgy. We sailed before lunch and as we sat down to it everything was normal till the pudding appeared on the table. It looked too stodgy for the Captain and without any more ado he shouted to the steward who appeared instantly.

'Steward,' he said, 'who made this pudding?'

'The cook, sahib,' said the steward.

'Tell the cook to come here.'

And presently the cook came into the saloon and salaamed very diffidently.

'Come right up here cook, and have a good look at this pudding you made.'

'The pudding very nice and good,' said the cook.

'Pudding, you call it, you old so and so. It is like lead!'

And with that he picked the crust off the apple pudding which easily came off and planted it right on the cook's face.

The northeast monsoon was on while we were "ploughing" our way up the China Sea and as usual the Captain worried about reefs, etc and bad weather and several times he had me out of my watch below to try and get star observations. In good weather he did not believe in the new fangled idea of having a star fixing of the ship. There was really nothing to worry about, but the old man always lost his nerve and became excited when navigating close to the land. For instance, during this voyage when we were approaching the Raffles Lighthouse in the Straits of Singapore a heavy tropical shower came on and he and the 2nd mate lost sight of the lighthouse. The Captain sent for me at once at 3pm when off watch and told me to go on to the forecastle and look out for the Raffles.

'Did you see the Raffles before the heavy rain came on?' I asked.

The Captain said, 'Yes, two or three points to the port bow.'

'Well,' I said, 'it will be impossible to hit it if you keep on the same course.'

'There you are,' he said, 'always optimistic.'

I went on to the forecastle head like a drowned rat, but shortly afterwards the shower passed and the Raffles Lighthouse appeared on the port bow as predicted. In due course we arrived safely in Shanghai. We left there for the Philippines, Cebu and Manila, to load copra, tobacco and cigars for Marseilles and Hamburg. When we had completed loading the stevedores gave me several boxes of the best cigars made in the Philippines. As I did not smoke, I brought these cigars home to my Father. I heard afterwards that he and several other old men in Toscaig enjoyed them very much, but they maintained that they enjoyed them much better if they cut them up and put them in their pipes.

We had an uneventful passage home. We met a sister ship bound east off Singapore. When we left the Philippines the weather did not look very promising, but it cleared up as we proceeded southwards, but the sister ship, the *"Baron Cawdor"*, which we met, got right into a cyclone just off the Philippines on its way to Shanghai. It blew a regular gale from the east for a day or so and the ship was at the mercy of the wind and waves, making no headway. Then, all of a sudden, they were in a dead calm, but within the hour the wind came out of the west and at one time they thought the ship was going under. The rails on the forecastle head were flattened out and heavy seas hit the bridge so the Captain and officers took shelter in an alcove behind the chartroom and the saloon stove funnel went through this alcove.

A terrific sea hit the bridge and the Captain put his arms round the funnel and said, 'Holy suffering Jesus, she is gone now.'

But she had not and the 3rd officer had the presence of mind to look round the fore and after decks. He found that one of the ventilators had gone overboard on the after deck and that the water was pouring down into the hold. He went to the carpenter's room. The carpenter, I believe, was a Chinaman and he said that it would be impossible to remain on deck to repair it and that they would both be washed overboard. The 3rd mate caught an axe which was in the room and shouted above the gale that he would kill him if he did not come out at once. So he jumped out at once and the 3rd mate took a bucket with him and he pushed it into the hole the ventilator left and, strange as it may appear, the bucket filled the hole to perfection so hardly any water could find its way into the hold of the ship. The 3rd mate, a MacDonald from Tiree, was a great friend of mine and sailed with me in the *"Baron Lovat"*. The ship was badly battered and, as the cyclone passed over them, they got into Shanghai crippled, but with no loss of life. The Captain's name was Goudy, a Nova Scotian, and my first voyage in the Baron steamers was with him from the U.S.A. to Honolulu.

In due course we arrived in Marseilles and discharged the bulk of the copra there, at least the portion of it that was not in bags and also about half the cargo in bags. As I was certain that the tallymen took more than was on the manifest of bags, I was sure there would be a shortage in Hamburg, so I got the crew down into the hold and filled some of the bulk copra into bags. I heard afterwards that we discharged an excess of bags in Hamburg. Consignees were always trying to rob other people's cargo and one had to be continually on the alert or else the ship would have to pay for shortages and the reputation of the chief mate suffered accordingly.

I must tell another story about Captain Bridger. On the way from the Messina Straits to Marseilles, the course was through the Straits of Ajaccio between Sardinia and Corsica. I was on watch the morning we were approaching the Straits and I got bearings of both Islands and plotted them in the chart. The Captain came on the bridge at about 8am so I told him of the bearing. The weather however, was a bit misty and he was doubtful of picking up the entrance. I, of course, was quite convinced that the visibility was not bad and that we could easily pick up the entrance and, as the Straits had deep water around them, it was easy navigation. The 2nd mate agreed with the Captain and they would not listen to me, so the course was altered to the north of Corsica, 100 miles extra on our route and next day we got in a gale and were delayed 24 hours.

While the Captain and I were arguing, he had said, 'When you get command you will pile your ship on the rocks through your optimism.'

In due course we arrived in Hamburg and later on to the Tyne for dry docking. Now I must admit that my memory lets me down for I missed a voyage out. In my last voyage where I said that we want to New York from Rio de Janeiro, actually we went from Rio to Tampa, Florida, and the voyage I had ended on the Tyne was to New York.

CHAPTER NINE

While we were on the Tyne there was the usual dry docking and loading coal for St. Vincent, Cape Verde. Nothing unusual happened on this passage and after discharging our cargo we sailed for Philadelphia. The Captain took flu and a heavy cold and took to his bed and I had to attend to him. He was so nice when he was in bed and praised me so much for giving such good attention. I got him on his feet after a great deal of reading the medical book which was in the medicine chest and by giving him freely all the medicine mentioned in the book. It is amazing how amateurs like me cured sailors. I presume, however, the good clean air at sea was more responsible for curing them than the medicine the ship carried. When we got to Philadelphia we heard of the disaster to the *"Titanic"*. We must have been well to the south of her on our course to Philadelphia so, as there was no wireless in those days, we never got any news till we got into port. We loaded case oil or two tins of paraffin in a wooden case for three ports in Japan. The voyage was uneventful till we left Moji and Nagasaki and came to a port on the west coast to discharge the remainder of our cargo. I think the name was Thurugi. It was the most primitive port I was ever in, although it was the terminal of the mail steamer from Vladivostok. Actually the mail steamer was at a pier several miles away from where we discharged our cargo. Women came on board to handle the cargo and do duty in the lighters. Indeed they appeared to me as if they were better workers than the men. We went back to Moji to load coal for Bombay. Here again the women worked in the lighters and handled the coal by taking it aboard in small baskets. Very often the women started duty by putting their babies in a sack (especially made) on their backs, but when their turn came to carry baskets of coal, the babies were left in their sacks on the deck of the lighters. When the day's work was done, the women took their clothes off and washed themselves in the sea. No modesty there. On the way to Bombay and while going through the Straits of Formosa we ran into dense fog. As usual the Captain kept on saying that we must reduce speed and I was, as usual, optimistic and kept on saying that we could see half a mile ahead. All of a sudden a thicker bank of fog came on us and just then we heard a noise of drums and tingling of bells, so we put the engines full speed astern. Great shouting coming from a junk as she was scratching her way alongside of us, but as our ship was almost stopped, no harm was done and the junk dropped astern in the fog. On arrival at Bombay we got orders to go to Karachi and load grain for Leith. Nothing much happened till we arrived at Karachi one afternoon when we were told that the holds were to be whitewashed to receive the cargo, so all hands were set to and this was accomplished before dawn the next day. No overtime in those days aboard ship.

I made three voyages to the Far East within two years and I never went ashore to have a look at the places we visited, at least east of Suez. One town was so like the other one that I just could not be bothered. Squalor and dirt everywhere and there were no cinemas or any places where a Britisher could enjoy himself. I was three weeks in Bombay at anchor in the harbour and during that time I had not been out of the ship. I have no doubt but that the Britishers in residence had a good time and had all the amenities necessary for full enjoyment. Their clubs were numerous and there were many other facilities for visiting each other and travelling around the country. They, of course, had their cliques and arranged themselves into classes, but the poor sailors had no friends except the pubs and, as I was an abstainer from the strong drink, these things did not appeal to me, however jovial the company. They very often became too jovial. Furthermore, there was such a lot of work, especially for the 1st mate, before the cargo workers stopped work and supper was served that I hadn't the inclination to gallivant ashore. Cash came into it, too. I was getting about £10 a month and, of course, my food, but then I required both tropical and winter clothing and something had to be saved to send to the old folk at home.

After a couple of week's loading at Karachi we left for Leith and the voyage home was uneventful. Going up the east coast of England got on the Captain's nerves as he thought navigation was fearfully difficult. I was so happy going to Leith and hopes of a few days at home that I suppose I was beaming with confidence and bragging about Edinburgh.

'Edinburgh,' he said, 'is famous for Ministers and Prostitutes.'

And he was angry going so far north. That night off Flamborough Head he sent for me in my watch below about midnight to say that he altered the course to the westward and he was sure error of the compass also altered. I got up to the bridge to find him very concerned. I pointed out to him that it was unusual for the deviation (compass error) to alter very much for a few points change in course.

'There you are again; can't you find out?'

The weather was hazy but the moon was out so I took a bearing of the moon to ascertain the compass error and it turned out as I expected, about 3 degrees, so all was well and I went to bed as my watch below was from 8pm to 4am. Captain Bridger so much hated to be near land and in narrow waters and very bad weather that he worked himself into a frenzy.

We got into Leith without a hitch and I was given a few days' leave. Captain Bridger was given promotion to a new ship and Captain Thomson from one of the sailing ships joined the *"Baron Ogilvy"*. Old Bridger would have liked me to accompany him but the office told him that it would be wiser for me to stay in the ship as Captain Thomson had no experience of steamships.

We left Leith for the Tyne (Newcastle) where some of the Leith cargo was to be discharged. I was back on board before the ship left for the Tyne. At Newcastle, after we discharged the cargo, we drydocked the ship.

We left the Tyne for Antwerp where we were chartered to carry a general cargo for Rio de Janeiro. We were not very long out of the Tyne on our way when I was called up to the bridge. I had been busy in the hold getting them all ready to receive the cargo immediately we arrived. Anyway, when I got up to the bridge, there was the Captain with the 2nd mate on the bridge going with the ship round and round a buoy. It was on one of the sandbanks on the East Coast of England. They both said that the flashes or description of the buoy did not correspond with the chart and that we must be on the wrong course. I ran down to the chartroom to consult the notices to mariners and there, sure enough, I discovered that the buoy was changed, so all was well and we proceeded on our course and in due time loaded our cargo and were on our way south. We called at Madeira for bunkers and when going into the harbour went in at too high a speed with the result that I had to let go both anchors to prevent our ramming a large German passenger ship. Sailing ships' masters were very often unable to grasp the speed of a ship driven by a screw until they got used to the working of the engines.

While we were discharging our cargo at Rio de Janeiro, the Captain took a slight stroke. I called the doctor in and he was sent to the fever hospital. It was a hospital put up by the British years and years ago when yellow fever was very prevalent in the Brazils. British ships were at that time very often lying in harbour unable to get a crew, their old crews either suffering from yellow fever or dead of it and I believe that was the reason for the erection of the hospital, but by 1912 there had been no cases of fever, so the Matron told me, for a long while. She was an Aberdonian and she said that the hospital was used for any sickness and the occupants were nearly all British, but at that time it was nearly empty. The doctors would not allow the Captain to return to work in the ship and it was arranged that he should be sent home by mail ship. Captain Bridger of the new *"Baron Jedburgh"* was unloading coal and he was very helpful. In about a week the Captain was put aboard a German liner for Southampton. On the way down from the hospital he told me to stop the taxi at a certain lottery shop as he was sure he had won something in the week's lottery. I took his ticket and, sure enough, he had won a prize but alas, it was for the week before. The bad boy who sold the ticket to the Captain must have known he was dealing in the wrong week.

After the liner sailed I had a cable from the owners to proceed to Buenos Aires to load wheat for Antwerp. This we duly did and nothing of importance happened till we reached Beachy Head where we stopped the Antwerp pilot boat. They were sailing smacks in those days. He agreed on the terms for pilotage and accepted the rate from the Bar to Flushing for the owners would not pay for anything else. After passing Dungeness Lighthouse it came on to blow from the NNW and within an hour or two we had a heavy gale and the ship was wallowing in a very heavy sea. When we reached the Bar Lighthouse next morning there were 9 large ships circling around as no pilot boats were able to face the gale. The wind abated somewhat and our pilot put up the flags "Follow me" so all the ships followed us over the Bar and up to Flushing. When the river pilot came on board and I said goodbye to the sea pilot, he said, 'I am now going to collect pilotage for the 10 ships.'

We left Antwerp within 10 days and sailed for Barry Docks where the ship was to load a full cargo outwards. While in Antwerp I had a letter from the owners to say that one of their oldest Captains was to relieve me in Barry Docks. This, of course, I understood, so after a smooth but very foggy passage to Barry I left the ship. Going up the Bristol Channel the fog cleared and we saw a Greek steamer in a sinking condition but with the Captain still on the bridge and with a small boat tied to the ship. The crew was all aboard one of the tugs or ships standing by to tow her to harbour, if possible. I don't think she survived the collision which she was in the night before, and she sank shortly after we passed her. I called at the office in Glasgow and told them that I was needing a holiday. Indeed for years I was only a few days per year at home for in those days if a sailor left his ship he had no guarantee that he could get another, however worthy he was of consideration. Shipowners did what suited them, especially tramp shipowners. I went home for at least a couple of months, which I enjoyed.

I got a telegram that I was appointed master of a steam ship of about 2,000 tons and was to join her in Cardiff. I stopped for a few hours in Glasgow to see the owners. I was told that my salary was to be £17 a month and that they had bought the ship from Furniss Withy and called her the *"Baron Blantyre"*. I was also told that they had made up my account for the *"Baron Ogilvy"* and that I owed them £30. They had had word from the charterers in Hamburg that they gave me a small commission of £30 for services rendered and for helping them in connection with the cargo, etc. I took it for granted that this money was my own and not the shipowners, but I had often heard rumours aboard all the ships I served in, that any commission the Captains received had to be handed back to the offices on their return to the U.K. or wherever the voyage ended. Shipmasters in those days were poorly paid but with all the little commission they got here and there, especially for turning out good cargoes which pleased the charterers they, of course, made a little on the side which helped to augment their pay. No doubt the system was often abused and mean shipmasters, for instance, got bad food and gear from foreign ship chandlers and in fact charged the shipowners for stuff that was never put aboard the ship. This irregular practice was not very common for the simple reason that any Captain who practised on a large scale got trouble from his crew and any shipowner who had any wisdom avoided it like the plague, for even in those days a happy ship and crew was of more importance to a master then anything else, especially on long voyages. Anyway, in my agreement to serve the firm as Master, it was stipulated that all commissions were to be handed over at the end of the voyage. It so happened that as the *"Baron Blantyre"* was on the Mediterranean run with coal out and either copper or iron ore home and the ship was stored for voyages of less than a month, the Captain received no commission, so there was none to return. I made several voyages in this ship and on the whole was quite happy in her, but some way or other I was disheartened. There appeared to be no security in the firm. Masters were often appointed without serving as mate or mates so promotion was difficult and, of course, officers would not stay and very often there was a change every voyage.

By the end of 1913 I arrived from Huelva with a cargo of copper ore and everything appeared as normal as usual, and we were almost loaded for the voyage outwards, when I was called to the office and was told that a new master was to join the ship and I was to go back as mate in one of their largest ships. I naturally protested as the master that was appointed came into the company as master a year before and I was nearly seven years with them. It was no use as the owners argued that I was the most junior master and that they counted the time from the day a man was appointed master and in any case three ships were sold and three masters were ashore and they even suggested, or at least it appeared that way, that I was lucky to get back as mate. I was extremely annoyed for I had a suspicion that the master appointed was a great friend of one of the Engineer Superintendents. There was no Marine Superintendent in the firm so there was no intermediary between the owners and the masters. By the end of the argument I could see no future in the firm so I asked them to be good enough to give me a reference, so the discussion ended and I was, as old sailors used to say "on the beach", but had an excellent reference.

To be "on the beach" was nothing very new to me as all the years I was before the mast I had to ferret a suitable ship for myself and was never very long ashore, looking for a ship. Now, however, I had a master's certificate and I was determined to get into a company of standing so, after taking lodgings in the same house as my brother, Murdo, who was a medical student in the University of Glasgow, I began hunting for a ship. My only difficulty was that if I joined a liner company I would have to join as 3rd mate with very slow promotion. I could join several firms on this basis, but came to the conclusion at long last to try for a good reliable firm. After several appointments at offices I went to Andrew Weir & Co - The Bank Line as it is now, but in those days they were mainly tramp shipowners but had several lines operating from India to South and North Africa. It meant long voyages, but on the other hand I was not married, so long voyages suited me as well as short ones. Their Engineer Superintendent was in the office so after a look at my references he told me that he was going to London that night and that he would hand my name over to the Marine Superintendent, Captain MacBride, and he would write to me.

In due course I got a letter from Captain MacBride who said that he had a vacancy for 1st mate in one of the bigger ships due within a few weeks and would I accept it, wages £14 a month, bed and bedding supplied. This was the first time in all my seafaring life that I got free bedding, etc, not even as master in the last ship and my wages as mate were not much lower than I had had as master. I decided to take the job. In about a week I had another letter to say the ship was diverted and was to carry troops to Mexico from the U.S.A. but Captain MacBride said that another of their large ships was due later on, if I would like to wait for her. Actually I had been ashore for some time and was getting restless and money was getting short. I therefore got a job as mate of a coaster for a time until the ship I was to join got home. In due course I left the coaster in Rochester after several voyages to the West Coast of Ireland (now Eire) and back. It was quite interesting going to seaports like Limerick and Yarmouth, etc. The only thing that I remember vividly was on a voyage from the West of Ireland to Whitehaven, with a light ship and we got into a strong head wind and put into Holyhead for shelter. I had never known of deep sea ships seeking shelter, but it was quite a good idea really for the ship could not make headway and to stay at sea was simply to waste coal. In deep sea ships the ship would have been "hove to". I remember when I was 3rd mate in the *"Baron Cawdor"* heaving to in the Pacific from Vancouver to Japan in 1908 in January. It was a full following gale and shortly after we hove to some of the lifeboats went overboard. My experience at that time convinced me that it would be more prudent to slow the engines down and keep the vessel's stern on the following wind and waves.

When I got the letter to join the *"Orteric"* in Rotterdam we were loading cement for Glasgow and the Captain of the coaster agreed to let me away or pay me off as done in all ships. I went to London and stayed with a friend of mine who used to be 2nd mate with me in the *"Baron Ogilvy"*. In a few days I was on my way to Rotterdam and was very pleased with my change of ships. We were there a couple of weeks before sailing for Galveston in the U.S.A. light ship. We got several of the apprentices from the sailing ships. The Bank Line were then selling their sailing ships at a quick rate; this was May 1914.

The Captain's wife and her daughter were aboard for the voyage. On arrival in Galveston, U.S.A., the cargo was not ready so we had a longer wait than normal and I suppose actually the delay was caused by the political situation in Europe as we were loading a full cargo for Hamburg. Captain Howie left us and joined the *"Kumeric"* which was almost loaded for Hamburg. I was sorry he left us and, as his wife was a very nice woman, I missed her and her daughter. The Captain of the *"Kumeric"* took over command of our ship. He was an extremely nice man but quite different from Captain Howie who took his responsibilities very seriously and the owners' interest was put above anything else, whereas the new Captain was gay and liked good company and having a good time; nevertheless he was a good seaman and attended to his work. When we were in Galveston, another of the ships came in there and the Bank Line's first tanker was in port a few miles above Galveston. It so happened that both the Captains of these ships were great friends of the Captain of our ship and they, of course, met every day and were having a good time. Sailors are notorious for that, I suppose, being cooped up in a ship for weeks on end generally makes them more convivial once they get on dry land. We started loading and as the stevedores in the U.S.A. are real go-getters, it did not take us long to put about 9,000 tons of wheat and 2,000 tons of cotton on board. The Captain had his fling the last night and I noticed when the pilot came aboard he was a bit unsteady on his feet and flushed in the face. Anyway, all went well and we put the ship on course and bound for Hamburg. The *"Orteric"* was one of the few ships outside the big liners that was fitted with wireless and I did not mention earlier that she was able to carry 12 first class passengers in very good berths and that she was able to carry large numbers of emigrants in her shelter deck, and beds were carried on board for that purpose. The Captain took to his bed after we left and, however much I tried, I could not get him out of bed. We were now coming down the coast of Florida and Key West and the course had to be altered to get through the Sound of Florida and to put the ship on a course for Cape Hatteras and Norfolk, Virginia, where we were to go for bunkers, sufficient to carry us to Hamburg.

I navigated the ship right round the coast of Florida, but still could not get any sense out of the Captain. Shortly before we got to Cape Hatteras, the Chief Engineer came to me and said that the Captain looked flushed and appeared to him to be very ill and that it would be advisable to get a doctor aboard on arrival in Norfolk. To this I agreed although I had my own private opinion that he was suffering from too much booze and had a private stock somewhere. In due course we got to Norfolk and when the Agent came on board I told him that the Captain was not well and to send a doctor aboard. When the doctor examined him he said he had enteric fever and that he would send an ambulance down at once to take him to the hospital. I was really taken flat aback at this and on the way to the gangway I said to the doctor that I thought that the Captain was drunk and that he had his own private stock which he had been consuming since we left Galveston.

'Well, Chief,' he said. 'I shall go back and have another look at him.'

In a few minutes he was back and said, 'Chief, I congratulate you on your right diagnosis of your Captain. Get the booze from him and you will have him on his feet soon.'

The Agent brought telegrams aboard from the owners and from the Admiralty to say that war was imminent and that I was to follow instructions. The Admiralty said that destroyers would meet us 100 miles west of Cape Clear and that no on account was I to pass Queenstown in South Ireland. I took a few minutes off to write to the owners and told them that the Captain was ill with fever and flu but I was sure he would be alright soon and that was the doctor's opinion who saw him. So we sailed before dark and that was the 3rd of August 1914 and I was neither worried nor very much concerned when the pilot left us and I set course for Queenstown. One thing did concern me, however, and that was to get the Captain back to work and good health. So after dark I asked the Chief Steward, a joyful Chinaman, how much gin and whisky, etc. were on board. He said three cases of gin and some whisky so I ordered all the booze on deck. He looked surprised but obeyed instantly. I suppose he thought it was something to do with the war the Europeans were organising. I called the 2nd mate along and told him I was dumping all the booze into the Atlantic. Before, however, committing it to the deep I took one bottle of gin out and told the steward to put it in my cabin.

Into the Atlantic went the booze and I said to myself, 'Now Captain, you will soon be sober.'

The 2nd mate was flabbergasted. Now that I had charge of all the drink aboard and no possible chance of the Captain getting any without my knowledge, he was bound to sober up sooner or later. He was not, however, reacting very well to my cure. Within three days the steward told him that he had no drink but that the Chief Officer had charge of it. By this time I was giving him a little out of my bottle and was diluting it more and more with water until one day he said that I was only giving him cold water.

One forenoon, as we were approaching the Newfoundland Banks, the wireless officer came running up to me to say that the German cruiser *"Konigberg"* (if I remember the name correctly) was chasing the *"Lusitania"*, the Cunard *"Flyer"*. I immediately plotted the position the *"Lusitania"* gave out on the chart and found we were only 30 miles away from them. Naturally, I wondered what to do to get away from them, but I decided to keep the course and trusted that they would not come our way. Presently we ran into a fog bank; the only time in my life I was glad to run into fog at sea, so we plodded along at about 11 knots and did not reduce speed for I was anxious to get away as far from the *"Konigberg"* as possible. Actually, I discovered afterwards she hurried south to Brazil. When the fog cleared there were no ships in sight and our voyage was going along smoothly and little by little I was getting the Captain back to his senses, although he was once or twice delirious and imagining he was seeing snakes climbing up the wall of his cabin. We were almost half way across the Atlantic and were nine days out from Galveston when on the morning watch at daybreak I saw a vessel with four funnels approaching us very fast. I recognised the ship although painted grey. She was the *"Aquitania"*, the big Cunarder and was flying Admiralty flags. She hoisted her flags to ask us to stop which I immediately did. We exchanged signals and she ordered us to proceed to Queenstown for orders so I rang down the engine room to go full speed ahead. As it was a lovely clear beautiful morning I left one of the apprentices on the bridge in charge and went down to see the Captain. He was much cheerier and asked me where we were. I said in the middle of the Atlantic, but he said that he heard the engine room telegraph ringing and that the ship stopped.

'Yes,' I said. 'A man 'o war stopped us.'

'A man 'o war,' he said, in a very sarcastic tone. 'And what damn right had he to ask you to stop?'

I said, 'There is a war on.'

'A war on,' said he. 'Don't be ridiculous!'

'It is true,' I said. 'Britain and Germany are at war and that ship was the *"Aquitania"* flying the white Ensign and already painted grey and on the Atlantic patrol.'

Talk about Rip van Winkle! After 100 years sleep he was not more surprised than our Captain.

'I am glad to see you much better,' I said. 'But you have had nothing to eat for about ten days now, so after breakfast I shall give you an emetic and as your bowels have not moved during the same period, I shall give you an enema.'

After breakfast I went into his cabin with a bowl of mustard and water. I said, 'Take this and that will clear the poison out of your stomach.'

He protested and said it was vile stuff and appealed to me not to give it to him, and said, 'For God's sake don't ask me to drink that!'

But after a great deal of argument I got him to take it and he was awfully sick and when he got over that I put him flat on the floor to give him the enema. I had really never given anyone this at sea or on shore, but I read very, very carefully the medicine book supplied with the medicine chest and carried out the instructions given to the best of my ability. But never having had any practice I suppose I was rough in administering it. I got the basin of warm water and added the soap and began operations with the instrument supplied. No sooner had I started than the Captain started to shout but I kept at the pump and I could see his tummy heaving up and down. At last I stopped and pulled the instrument out and never did I see such a mess; I had pumped so much into the poor man that the force of what came out hit the roof of the cabin. After a few hours of good rest the Captain dressed, had lunch with us and took over the command of the ship as if nothing had happened and we proceeded on our voyage. We met a destroyer which took us into Queenstown and we anchored half way up to Cork and there lay for about a week enjoying the Irish scenery. Then we got orders to go to Liverpool to discharge. Nothing much happened while there and after finishing the discharge of our wheat and cotton which, of course, the British Government confiscated, we stored the ship, dry docked her and proceed light to Calcutta.

The Captain went down to the office in London and they were all very sorry for him for having such a bad illness on the way home. I did not get home as there was little time to go anywhere while the ship was in port. It did not take us long to get to Port Said and we made quick progress and speed with a light ship. We were, however, delayed at Port Said as the Canal Company refused to allow ships through unless the Canal dues were paid in gold. So this new arrangement took time and in the meanwhile the other ship that was with us in Galveston arrived and with the same old cheery Captain. He enticed our Captain (who was easily led) ashore and they were having, as usual, a good time. Word came on board that we were to pass through the Canal next morning. The Captain, I could see, had had more than enough again and I don't know even now how he and the 2nd mate and 2nd engineer got together on the way through the Canal, but by the time we got to Suez and had to anchor for the Agents to get aboard with our clearance, they were all jolly. In a matter of minutes the all clear was given to us to proceed and I went forward to heave the anchor up, but I noticed from the forecastle head that the Captain and 2nd mate were acting a bit queerly in getting the ship's position right for proceeding south on our course through the channel for the Gulf of Suez. I immediately went on the bridge to see for myself what was going on. The 2nd mate met me at the head of the stairs and assured me that he was assisting the Captain to get the ship on her course. I said, 'the blind leading the blind', and as before took over the bridge till we got well down the Gulf of Suez and both the 2nd mate and Captain went to bed. The 2nd mate was able to take his watch at midnight, but I am sorry to say that the Captain put in no appearance next morning and he was on the same old "tack" again, and he was not himself for about four days and by this time we were passed Perim and in the Arabian Sea. The Red Sea navigation is pretty intricate so I was much more concerned than in the Atlantic and I suppose I had to get up in my watch below to see that things were going right and alter the course if necessary. Anyway, everything went all right but I was glad to be out of the Red Sea. We were not long getting to Calcutta and on arrival there were told that the Indian Government had taken the ship in charter to carry horses from Australia to Calcutta. So minor alterations were made for this purpose but the main ones were to be done on our arrival in Melbourne. We also loaded some cargo for Melbourne.

Meantime, an old shipmate was also in Calcutta, so the "Boys" got together again to have a good time and a good time they had and, of course, our Captain being a very nice man had so many friends in Calcutta that by the time we left he was as bad as ever, and took the precaution of having more drink aboard. Navigation from Calcutta to Melbourne is very easy as practically a direct course can be set from the mouth of the Ganges to Cape Leeuwin, Western Australia. I therefore did not worry overmuch. When we got a short distance off the Cocos Island we picked up on the wireless a message that the Australian cruiser *"Sydney"* had been chasing a German raider and, if I remember rightly, had got her, so that was a load off our minds.

The Captain, in spite of my efforts, was not getting back to normal and one evening after coming off watch I called on him as usual. He was very depressed and ready to die and told me what letters and photos to destroy and, if he got worse, I was to alter course so that he could be buried in Geraldton, Western Australia. By this time he was again seeing snakes, etc. I told him not to be silly and to go to sleep. I went to sleep myself but at 2am I thought I heard some movement on the bridge and that the course was altered. I got up and went up on the bridge and there was the 2nd mate on watch and the ship on a course to Geraldton.

'Why did you alter course?' I asked, to which he replied that the Captain came up on the bridge and told him to alter the course.

'How dare you alter the course without instructions from me. Put her back on the old course at once!'

So he did and we continued on this course, but in a day or two the Captain got back to normal so he and I had a heart to heart talk, with the result that he swore that he would not touch drink again, and no one was more surprised than our Australian Marine Superintendent, Captain Lowe, when he and our Captain went into a hotel for a drink and found our Captain drinking lemonade. He kept his word and never drank again while he was in the ship with me.

The whole ship was more or less gutted out to make stalls for horses on our arrival at Melbourne and coal ballast was put into the lower holds and a platform of wood on top of it so that we could carry horses on four decks, that is in the lower holds on the platform mentioned, on the twin decks and the shelter deck and the main deck forward of the bridge and aft of the engine room, so we had the capacity to carry over 2,000 horses altogether.

We discovered a fire in our forward coal bunkers before arrival in Melbourne, but though we thought we could easily deal with it ourselves we had to get the Fire Brigade. The Harbour Authorities were annoyed and said that we should have reported the fire before we got into the harbour. They had to pump tons of water into No. 2 hold before they were satisfied that the fire was extinguished.

On completion of our alterations we went to Newcastle to embark our horses which we got to Calcutta without serious losses. The Calcutta authorities were very pleased with the condition of all the horses and our small losses on the trip. We had to engage Australian cattlemen to look after the horses and they were a tough crowd and we also had an Australian carpenter to repair the stalls, etc. He was the first communist I ever met and this was the end of 1914. A very nice chap, but made "Gods" of Karl Marx and Lenin and at that time very few of the working classes knew anything about the theories of those two.

One of the cattlemen came to me one evening to tell me he had very bad toothache and would I pull the tooth out. I got the Captain to examine it and we decided, as he insisted, to pull it out. We had him sitting on the edge of the bath in the Captain's bathroom. (As I mentioned somewhere already, the medicine chest in all cargo ships was installed in the Captain's bathroom.) The Captain took the forceps and I held the man's head. After a great deal of discussion about whether we had the right tooth, the Captain pulled and I held on firmly and the man yelled, but the tooth came out. Next morning I called on him to see if everything was alright. He said that we had pulled out the wrong tooth and he was not going through the same experience again, but he felt better all the same.

We made another trip to Newcastle and back to Calcutta. We dry docked in Sydney before going on to Newcastle, so had a couple of days there which I enjoyed as I was able to see my aunt. Her husband was my mother's brother, Norman MacLennan. I also saw her son and daughter. My uncle had died in 1910. We got Indians in Calcutta to replace the Australians who were looking after the horses. The Australians were needed at home, but the carpenter remained with us. The trip down to Australia was a busy time for me, and the ship had to be whitewashed wherever there were stalls, and I used to make the Indian cattlemen work the fore part of the ship and the Chinese crew the other part of the ship and when they met they quarrelled and on one occasion fought and there was I, in the middle of the fight to pacify them. I used to be so desperate to get the work finished that I pushed the clock on in the middle of the night so as not to lose time during the day. From the Leeuwin to Newcastle we normally gained half an hour going east so I got an extra half hour out of the men and when we were going west I put the clock back at 11am so I therefore got an extra half hour again. There are tricks in every trade.

We weren't long in getting back to Calcutta where we got orders that our next trip was to Marseilles, France, with a full load of horses. The Captain told the Navy Board in Calcutta that the coal ballast that was in the lower holds would have to be taken out, as all the horses' urine was draining into the bottom of the holds and the bilges and that the ship was beginning to stink and this would have an effect on all the horses on a long voyage to France. Reluctantly, they agreed to discharge all the ballast coal and sent us to the Nicobar Islands, a Penal Settlement, where the job was to be done. There were no facilities there to do the job quickly and all the labour was done by convicts and work was spasmodic, so we had a longer time than we expected. Not a very pleasant place to be in, but we were able to take walks here and there in the country which was pleasant enough, but we were not allowed off the ship after dark. We eventually sailed after a wait of about 10 days and went this time to Thursday Island and the Great Barrier Reef, a change from Cape Leeuwin and the South of Australia where winter gales were beginning.

Before arriving we had a message from the Sanitary Authorities in Newcastle that the ship would not get a berth till all the fresh water (that is, drinking water) was pumped out and fumigation carried out. These were very difficult instructions to carry out, especially if we had a mishap to our engines at sea and found ourselves without fresh water. Anyway, the pump that delivered water to the galley and other parts of the ship was only a small handpump, so it was quite a business to try and empty a tank which normally held several tons of water. The Captain was desperate to get ashore and so were other officers and engineers. The sulphur stink pots were arranged through all the decks, as the ship was to be fumigated from stem to stern. All hands were taking turns at the pump, but they were having very little effect on the amount of water in the tank. It was getting near lunch time and I could see that it would take us hours to get the tank empty, so I got one of the Chinese crew to go down into the tank and keep the palm of his hands dead below the hole which the sounding rod went through and just above the water. The Chinaman went down as ordered and sat very innocently on his hunkers in the water. The Sanitary Inspector came along and sounded the tank and, lo and behold, the end of the rod was dry, so everybody shouted that the tank was dry so word went along the deck to light the stink pots with the sulphur in them. Meantime the Sanitary Inspector said to me that when he lowered the rod into the tank, it seemed to hit something soft and not the steel bottom of the tank, and he thought he would have a look into the tank, and what did he see but the Chinaman. He was so angry that he could not talk and as the fumes of the sulphur were now beginning to permeate the space round the tank, he could only splutter and cough and I was only worried about how to get the Chinaman out of the tank, but the bosun and other members of the crew were soon on the job. Actually, it took us quite a while before we got him out and we all got up on the main deck, but none of us were the worse for our ordeal. The Sanitary Inspector and his staff left us at once, the Inspector full of fury, but I never heard any more about it. I suppose the Inspector realised that there was not much water in the tank and considering that the full complement of the ship had been drinking it for a couple of weeks and was none the worse for it, it could not do the Australians much harm. The members of the crew and the Captain walked ashore and there the matter ended.

We were not long in getting our quota of horses aboard and I imagine that the farmers did not much care what kind of horses they sold for shipment to France. They appeared to me (although I knew nothing about horses) to be inferior to the two other shipments. It was again decided to go through the Great Barrier Reef and keep in the good weather round the north of Australia as the Captain thought the bad weather we were bound to get would have a very bad effect on the horses and might wash those on the main deck with their stalls overboard. We had many losses on the voyage to France, about 107 altogether, but the Army service people in Marseilles thought we had quite a good record. However, I presume that by this time, March/April 1915, the Army authorities had convinced themselves that horses were not of much use in trench warfare. I often heard Army people talking about the day when the British Cavalry got into the German Army and smashed them up.

Whatever the reason, we were told in Marseilles that the ship was to be released and go back on to the owners trade, so we left Marseilles and got orders to go to Calcutta to load for the Argentine.

I am also quite sure that the owners were happy as freight rates jumped enormously during the time the ship was on charter to the Indian Government. The Argentine run was one of the regular runs of the owners, but owing to the high freight rates prevailing, I believe our cargo of gunny sacks, tea, etc (mostly sacks), cost as much to take to the Argentine as the ship cost to build a few years earlier; on the other hand, the cost of fuel, stores, etc, went up in the same proportion.

We loaded a full cargo - not an empty corner in the ship - and sailed round South Africa, calling at Durban and Cape Town for bunkers. I met my cousin Kenneth MacDonald in Cape Town. He was Chief Officer in the *"City of Athens"* and was promoted to Master on a captured German ship. We had a good passage across the South Atlantic, although it was the month of August when bad weather is expected there. We were a couple of weeks in Buenos Aires and got orders to go to the west coast of South America to load a cargo of nitrate for Alexandria, Egypt. It was pleasant weather going through the Straits of Magellan and in no time we got to Pisagua and Antofagasta where we loaded our cargo.

Just before we left Pisagua we got orders to sail back through the Straits of Magellan as there was a subsidence in the Panama Canal and our ship was much too big to pass through - or so at least the Canal authorities thought. One of the company's ships the *"Poleric"* actually reached Panama on the way home and she was not allowed to enter the canal, with the result that she had to return down the west coast of South America and get home via the Magellan Straits. We were disappointed, but this was nothing compared with the ship that actually reached the Canal. Anyway, we proceeded according to orders and got through the Straits in good clear weather in November, early summer down there. By 1914 the Magellan Straits were buoyed and lighted in the narrow parts. One night while passing the narrowest channel in the Straits, with high cliffs on one side and a lighted buoy on the other side on a reef, the night was very dark and the Captain and I were on the bridge. All of a sudden we heard a terrible roar and we really thought the ship was going over the reef, but in a few seconds we realised that a big whale had spouted a few yards from us. Sailors imagine all sorts of things in the dark.

CHAPTER TEN

Owing to our diversion round the south coast of South America we had not sufficient bunkers to take us to Oran which was our original coaling port on our way to Alexandria. We had to call at Montevideo for bunkers. While we were coaling there a large black cat came aboard and this cat came out every night from his hiding place and made an awful mewing, with the result that it woke up everyone as it wandered about the deck. We tried every possible way to catch him and tame him, but he defied us. Eventually we put into Oran, North Africa, for bunkers and, while there, I got the crew to clear and wash out two big houses in the fore deck. Just as the coal lighters were leaving the side of the ship with all the lumpers aboard, did not some of the crew find the black cat hiding! They grabbed him and threw him overboard. The 3rd mate, who was a Shetlander, was speaking to me on the bridge deck at the time and he got foaming mad at the idea of throwing a black cat overboard, especially in war time. I must admit I never heard any superstition about black cats in the Highlands and Highlandmen were about the most superstitious people in Britain when I was a boy. Who arrived aboard then, but the Captain and he noticed that the 3rd mate was very agitated and asked what was the matter. So he told him the end of the black cat. The Captain belonged to Fife and, of course, he got into the same state as the 3rd mate and they were both inclined to blame me for allowing the crew to do such a dastardly act. I pleaded innocence as the cat was in the water before I knew anything about it. In any case one of the men in the lighter had saved the cat and I hoped now that he was being cared for in a good home. Some of the engineers were also worried about the affair. The Captain told me about his experience in one of the ships in the Pacific. The ship went on her beam end and it took them days to get her righted. At times they thought that the ship would turn turtle as she was so badly listed. They had a Chinese crew and some one in the ship threw a cat overboard a day or two before the gale.

I said, 'But you saved the ship and yourselves.'

'Yes,' he said, 'but it was a damned near thing.'

Some time afterwards he told me that the cat was white and in some parts of China it was a white cat which brought luck, and on that occasion it was the Chinese crew who made all the fuss of how ill luck would come through the cat going overboard.

There was some gloom amongst the British officers and engineers when we departed that night from Oran. We were sailing without lights at night which made navigation hazardous. We were, of course, following the usual shipping lanes in the Mediterranean, but had been warned at Oran that German submarines, based on the Adriatic, were sinking ships in the Eastern Mediterranean. As we passed Malta in daylight, it would have been very easy to have a patrol ship on guard to warn us to keep either south or north of the usual route to Port Said or Alexandria. We increased speed from 11 to 12½ knots which the ship could easily do. Looking back after all these years with the Second World War intervening, I can't understand why we were so stupid ourselves as not to go south of Malta and hug the North African coast where submarines would not go to look for ships to sink. I presume we were a bit casual and imagined our speed would safeguard us. Anyway, we just carried on, on the usual lane, and no sight of any Admiralty vessels to warn us. The Navy was for fighting and not guarding merchant ships and if a few merchant ships were lost, that was not of much consequence. But the "Powers That Be" in those days had to alter their opinions later on when they realised that nearly half of the British Mercantile Fleet was in Davy Jones' Locker.

We were doing a good 12½ knots when, about 240 miles from our destination, I saw as daylight came at about 6am lifeboats on our port bow. I immediately altered course to see if any men were aboard. They were empty, just floating about on the wide ocean. This was a warning to us, but again we resumed our old course. The Captain was on deck the whole afternoon watch, for some reason or other he had little faith in the 2nd mate. A few days before I had gone up on to the bridge to deposit the scrap logbook in the charthouse and saw the 2nd mate still in the corner of the bridge with his face quite pale.

I said, 'What is wrong with you?'

To which he replied that he saw a torpedo coming straight for us.

'You saw,' said I, 'dolphins coming straight at us.' For I had seen them playing about and playing tricks a minute earlier from the lower bridge.

I went below and had an hour's sleep and was on duty on the bridge again at 4pm and ordered the crew to put the finishing touches on what they were doing, painting, etc as we were expected to reach Alexandria early next morning.

The Captain said to me, 'As you are here now I shall go below and have a bath.'

A few days before this the Captain said to me that he had thirty gold sovereigns in his cabin, but he said, 'I am putting them now in my pocket in case we have to leave the ship in a hurry and I forget about them. Be sure if you have any to do the same.'

I had a mere three sovereigns and I duly stowed them away in my waistcoat pocket. After the Captain left me, I was walking up and down the bridge, congratulating myself on how I had got the ship into a spick and span condition with all the painting done. All of a sudden I saw a spout of water going up on the port bow and I thought to myself, 'that is a big whale'. Then almost immediately I saw another and I could see a long black thing on the horizon, so I took the binoculars to have a look at it. Then and only then I realised it was a submarine firing at us. I put the helm hard over and put our stern on her, sent a message to the Captain who was in his bath by one of the apprentices and phoned down to the 2nd Engineer, who was on duty, to put on best speed possible as a submarine was after us. He replied that he was cleaning fires and was losing speed. Fires had to be cleaned out every four hours in the "good old days" when coal was the motive power in all ships. I shouted to the Bosun to take his men down to help the 2nd Engineer in the stokehold. By this time the Captain was on the bridge, busily employed pushing his shirt into his trousers. Also the Chief Engineer came up on to the bridge. Just then a shell hit the windlass and smashed it up. Further shells came aboard aft but they were not all hitting the ship. There was nothing much we could do. We could not retaliate as no guns were on board. The boats were all ready on the davits and could be put into the water in a few minutes. All I remember about this time is that I went into my cabin to put a heavy uniform jacket on and heavier shoes on and went back on to the bridge where the Captain told me that he was going down to his cabin to throw overboard the Admiralty code book we had on board. Later on, when he got back, I went along the boat deck to see that all was ready in case we had to abandon ship. The rods for the steering gear came along the main aft deck, but whether a shell had struck them or not I don't know, but the ship took a sheer to starboard and as she was now in a position to have a torpedo put into her, the Captain gave the order to abandon ship and stopped her so we all went to our respective boats. I put my crew aboard the boat, taking charge of the boat falls myself and telling one of the apprentices to attend to the after falls. We lowered the boat very carefully and, as I noticed there was a little way still on the ship, I gave strict orders to the man at the forward fall not to let them go till I was aboard. Just before this a shell hit the Captain's boat and some of the crew were killed and some wounded, so the wounded men were dragged across the deck and put into my boat (I think five of them). Meantime, the Chief Engineer and the 3rd mate were away in their boat, and I actually thought the Captain, 2nd Engineer and wireless operator were in the boat that got away. I ordered the apprentice standing by the after falls to slide down the falls and go into the lifeboat and I was just going to do likewise when the men in the boat let go and I would have to jump and swim for it for the boat was a bit away from the ship. Just then, however, I looked over my shoulder and there were the Captain, 2nd Engineer and wireless officer, who had missed getting in the 3rd mate's boat, and were coming over to get into mine.

We all went to the jolly boat and started lowering it into the water. I was at the forward falls and the Captain at the after falls. The 2nd Engineer and wireless officer were in the boat. I jumped on the falls to lower myself into the boat, but the same thing happened as in the lifeboat. The 2nd Engineer let go the falls. Luckily he got hold of the boat hook and I caught it and pulled the boat to me and jumped into it. We decided to move away from the ship and it is as well we did for the submarine put a torpedo into her and it did not take long to sink her as the holds were full of empty spaces as nitrate is a very heavy cargo. Actually she went down in a few minutes and there we were left on the ocean in a small jolly boat. Luckily for us the submarine came down to where we were and they insisted on seeing the Captain and he was ordered aboard. We rowed to the side of the submarine and there two sailors with revolvers stood and told him to go to the bridge where the Captain wanted him. Naturally he was taken aback, but obeyed instantly when the revolvers were pointed at his head. At the bridge he was questioned and had to give details of the ship and her cargo. Meantime, we lay alongside the submarine and the 2nd Engineer, who was in his boiler suit, said to me that if he could only get a few cigarettes or a pipeful of tobacco he would not be so miserable. I whispered to him to ask the sailors on the side of the submarine for a few cigarettes.

'No,' he said. 'I am afraid to ask them for anything.'

So I spoke to them, saying that my friend was dying for a cigarette. Their reply was a handful of cigarettes and a plug of tobacco. Meantime, the Captain came down the ladder and we were naturally glad that they did not keep him aboard. By this time we were a long way from the lifeboats and it would soon be dark and the Captain of the submarine thought that some of the crew were drowning amongst the little wreckage floating about where the ship went down. I told him that some men were killed before we had left the ship and all those alive were in the boats. We ourselves were very close to the ship before she went under and we would have seen if any men were in the water. The men killed and wounded had been sitting in the Captain's boat when a shell went through it and as I helped to put the wounded men in my own boat, I was certain no one alive was left on board. I suggested to our Captain that he should ask the Captain of the submarine to tow us to our respective lifeboats as we had no food or water in the boat we were in. The Captain told me quietly that they had him on the "mat" already and he was not going to ask any favours. I then plucked up the courage to shout to the Captain of the submarine to tow us to the lifeboats.

'Where are they?' he asked.

To which I replied, 'On your starboard bow.'

'Hang on,' he said, and he towed us to our boats about a couple of miles away. He was a decent chap after all.

When I got into my boat I found either four of five wounded men and I decided to try to bandage them somehow, but as there were no bandages in the lifeboat or any other medical appliances, it was very difficult to know how to start; but I do remember tearing the lining of my jacket for the first man I tackled, who had a very bad wound on his leg, and some way or other I got him stretched out and more comfortable. Then I happened to look up and saw the lights of a ship coming our way, answering the signals the other lifeboats put up. This was the P&O ship *"Moldavia"*, now a hospital ship bound for Alexandria and Gallipoli. Her lights were blazing, of course. She stopped and all the boats (three in all) smartly rowed alongside of her. My boat was the last to get there, but the men in the other two boats must have known there were wounded men in my boat for, by the time we got to the gangway of the *"Moldavia"*, there were doctors and nurses standing by with stretchers, etc and my five wounded men were taken down to the operating table immediately and I am glad to say they all recovered. We got a meal immediately we got aboard which we enjoyed.

The ship sank about 5pm and we were safely aboard the *"Moldavia"* by 8pm. While we were at dinner the Captain told me that he had such a rush jumping out of the bathroom when I sent the apprentice down to him to say that a submarine was after us that he left his waistcoat with the thirty sovereigns in the pocket in the bathroom.

'A great loss,' I said, 'but you ought to be thankful you are not in the submarine, a prisoner of war.'

The Captain was given a berth for the night in the room of the Captain of the *"Moldavia"* and all of us got good berths. The excitement over, I fell asleep right away and did not waken up till 7.30 in the morning.

I did not mention the weather. In fact the sea was like a millpond with just a gentle westerly breeze; even the lifeboats did not roll.

After we had breakfast we met on deck. The Chief Engineer told me he did not sleep a wink but that most of the other officers and engineers slept all right.

The Captain told me that he also did not sleep a wink, but he said, 'I will tell you something. You remember my telling you after dinner last night that I left my waistcoat and the thirty sovereigns in the bathroom?'

'Yes,' I said, 'and I am very sorry for you, and through your advice I have my three sovereigns in my waistcoat pocket now.'

'Well, listen to this, when I was taking my clothes off last night I could not understand what was the hard thing next to my skin under my shirt and, lo and behold, when I looked it was my waistcoat, so when I jumped out of the bath it was my waistcoat I grabbed first!'

'Just,' said I, 'what a man from the Kingdom of Fife would do.'

Aboard the *"Moldavia"* were two other crew which had had their ships sunk earlier than us the same day. One of them was a Greek. The crew, after they had abandoned their ship, were picked up by a small ship belonging to the Cunard Line. Within three hours the submarine sank the Cunard boat so there was hardly enough room in the lifeboats for the two crews. These two crews abandoned ship when the submarine put a shot across their bows.

We arrived in Alexandria at 2pm and as we left the *"Moldavia"*, the Army aboard and the officers and crew of the ship cheered us.

We got lodgings in some broken down hotel but we were quite happy so next morning we trooped along to see the British Consul. We were not very cordially received. The 2nd Engineer, who was still going about in a boiler suit, wanted more money than the £3 the Clerk in the Consulate offered us to rig ourselves out with, for all the clothes we had were what we stood in. The 2nd Engineer and the 4th, who was an Australian, commenced an argument about the niggardly sum offered us to make ourselves presentable, even to the man in the street. As the argument heated up there were shouts that we wanted to see the British Consul. In my young days at sea the British Consul was a sort of mythical figure who had the power to settle all arguments and be fair and just to all sailors in any quarrels between the Captain or owners with their crews. Many a profound argument I listened to in the forecastle of the various ships I served in on the duties of the British Consuls in foreign countries. Sailors called them British Councils. I noticed, however, in those days that the Consuls were more inclined to listen to the shipowners and captains and side with them than the poor sailors. I even heard one of them saying that however much money you gave sailors they went out and pissed it against the wall, in other words, they spent all their wages in the pubs.

To get back to the arguments in Alexandria, the Consul did put in an appearance and he was to me a fierce looking individual with an eye glass and as far as he was concerned we were all distressed British seamen and he would deal with us as such and get a passage for us as soon as possible homewards so, with our tails between our legs, we departed gladly with our £3 each. There was not much humanity there.

But I was better off than the others as I had my three golden sovereigns still stowed away in my waistcoat pocket. I had bought a flannel suit in Calcutta before sailing from there to South America and I had never liked it, so sold it to the 3rd Engineer who was an Aberdonian. He had been wearing it for about three months so I told him that he should pay me for it.

'No fear,' he said, 'it is now at the bottom of the ocean and if you had not sold it to me it would still be at the bottom of the ocean.'

So I never got paid for it. I really did not expect it. We eventually got £50 each for all the clothes we lost; the Board of Trade made the rule.

We were hanging around Alexandria for days and no money to spend and having arguments every day how to spend our £3. I spent it on underclothing and a pair of shoes.

Meantime, the Captain was trying to get in touch by cable with the owners. He saw the agents and before we got away the owners advised the agents to advance us money. Actually we all had quite a good amount to our credit as we had been away from the U.K. for over a year. We never went to the Consulate again for we all imagined that the officers of the Cunard boat received better treatment than us. Possibly they did as the Cunard Line was well known. I saw the Chinese crew before they left for the East and they agreed with the Captain and the 3rd mate that those who lost their lives through the shelling of the lifeboat, while launching it, were those responsible for throwing the black cat overboard at Oran.

The Captain got a direct passage through Italy to the U.K., but we were all put aboard the P&O *"Malta"*, 2nd class. She was a cargo boat carrying a small number of 1st and 2nd class passengers. My cabin was at the very stern of the ship and had a small skylight over it, and the first time the gun that was fitted on the deck above in Port

Said was fired for practice, all the glass in the skylight came down on top of me in bed and I was after that placed in a 1st class cabin which was more comfortable. The *"Malta"* was loaded with iron ore which made her roll violently and off Cape Finisterre, on Christmas Eve 1915, she had to be hove to in one of the worst gales I was ever in. The 20 year old ship rolled so much that three times during the night I was rolled out of the bunk on to the floor.

We were in London in a few days and I was in Glasgow on New Year's Day where I spent my £50 on clothes.

My brother Murdo, who was in the Camerons as a Captain, also arrived in Glasgow the same day. My brother John was also there. He was later on in a minesweeper in Peterhead. We decided to travel north together. Murdo had a 1st class ticket all the way home, so had I, so between us we paid or exchanged 3rd class for 1st for John and we were all together in the same carriage. We never travelled 1st class before on the railways. Indeed we were always thankful to have sufficient money to travel 3rd class. We wired Aunt Jessie, Kinlochewe to accompany us to Applecross. She was my mother's sister. She was married to a John Murchison, a retired gamekeeper, who became a prosperous farmer, but they had not a family. Sure enough, when the train got to Achnasheen, there was Aunt Jessie looking into all the 3rd class compartments. The stationmaster told her (he knew her well) that her nephews were travelling 1st class. By this time we were on the platform. She foamed and raved at us for travelling 1st class.

'How dare you do such a thing!' She shouted, but in the end we bundled her in.

She was so cross at us that she could not talk of anything else but extravagant young men and waste of money and to make matters worse John agreed with her, not meaning it of course, but my brother John is full of humour and always was; at home whenever he saw Father and his sister Aunt Ann having an argument, he never hesitated to add fuel to the flames to keep things moving. Aunt Jessie, of course, was famous for her horror of extravagance and in her ways and habit she was thrifty and careful with money, although very generous in her house. She dressed well, but I should think her dresses would last a long time and she was as careful of them as of money. She had a lot of money saved, which was her own, for she made it in the Island of Jura where her husband was the head gamekeeper. She had a number of cows and sold butter and milk; the yacht in the bay was her best customer. My brother Murdo kept on asking her to let him have his share of her money as it was unlikely he would survive for long in the trenches in France and he would like very much to enjoy it then. She even then had not made a will but she had no near relations except us five brothers and her nephew and niece in Australia.

Time flew past in the train and steamer to Applecross. Who was on leave at home but our brother, Roderick. He was 2nd mate of a steamer, the *"Crewe Hall"*, and their ship was sunk east of Malta, about 120 miles, in a strong north-easterly wind. They had all got out of her with most of their belongings. In fact the carpenter took his tool chest in the 3rd mate's boat. At about 3pm the Captain told Roderick that he had better go into the 3rd mate's boat because he had more experience of sailing small boats.

So we had; as boys in Applecross we sailed small boats as early as I can remember. In fact it was the only means of conveyance to the railhead, except over the road (2,110 feet to the summit!). Immediately Roderick got aboard his boat in the afternoon, he ordered the Lascar crew to lie in the bottom of the boat and threw the carpenter's tool box overboard. He then set the sail and steered a course for Malta and, as the lifeboat he was in had finer lines than the other lifeboats, because she was used for taking the Captain ashore, if they were loading or discharging in any of the Roadsteads that surround the coast of India, she sailed well. In the morning they sighted Malta and were picked up later on. The strong favourable wind speeded them along and he stayed at the helm himself all night. The two lifeboats got lost and they were at sea for 8 days before they were picked up. Roderick's ship was lost about ten days before ours so he was home before us.

The whole family was at home except Kenny who was in Gallipoli. This was the first week of January 1916. Murdo was the first to leave for he had only a week's holiday from France. Roderick a few days after got a telegram to join one of the Hall Line ships. When we four brothers were all at home together lots of folk used to come in every evening to Ceilidh, an old custom in the Highlands, and we mostly argued and talked about the war. Most of us were optimists and agreed it would be over within six months. Some gave their reasons and the most popular one was that the Germans would die of starvation owing to the Blockade by the Navy. Father doubted this very much so everyone turned on him. Well, he would say, my reason is this: for nearly a year now everyone said that the Germans were reduced to eating ferns and rushes, but nevertheless, they win battles and claim victories, so they can't be on the edge of starvation. How right he was! Nearly all the old men and women in the village at that time spoke only Gaelic and could not read or write, but, nevertheless, had strong opinions of their own and had a wonderful grasp of geography. Their children and some grandchildren were in the Ross Mountain Battery which was fighting in the Near East.

Meantime I had a letter to say that I was appointed Chief Officer of the S.S. *"Salamis"* which was on a regular run from Japan and China to South African ports and my passage to Durban was booked on the *"Kennilworth Castle"* sailing in about a week's time. So I now had to start packing.

My brother John played a trick on Roderick which amused us all. Like me Roderick had to buy lots of clothes after he lost everything when his ship was sunk. Roderick had several pairs of new shoes and John asked him several times to leave a pair with him, but he refused. Then the night before he left Roderick had to go out to say goodbye to all his friends and asked John to pack his sailor's bag for him, which he willingly did. When Roderick got to Bristol and unpacked his bag there was one shoe missing, so Roderick sent back the shoe which was, of course, of no use to him and told John he did it on purpose. We all then knew why John was so willing to pack Roderick's bag, and what is more, he admitted to us he did it on purpose: he called it a joke.

When I left Aunt Jessie came with me and I went to Kinlochewe for the night. When we got to Achnasheen the train from the south was very late so, as the mail coach had to wait several hours for the train to arrive, I decided to take a taxi to Kinlochewe. But it would cost 10/- so Aunt Jessie said we would walk it - 10 miles! I refused point blank, but she said she could buy 3lbs of tea for 10/-. Finally I won my point and we hired. She, of course, was as usual very gracious and kind in her house. Her husband had died about a year before and she had her brother-in-law with her, also his daughter. Next day I had to hire again to catch my train for London. After a few days in London, we embarked on the Castle Liner in Tilbury. A new Chief Engineer, 2nd Engineer and 2nd mate embarked with me, in early February.

When we were passing the Goodwin Sands at 3pm and at low water a lady passenger came to me as I was having my usual walk on deck and asked me quite seriously if that long black streak on the horizon was a German submarine, to which I replied, 'No, Madam, that is the Goodwin Sands.'

'Oh,' she said. 'I am happy it is not a submarine.'

The ship was crowded with passengers and we were travelling 2nd class which was comfortable and we had a pleasant journey to Durban where we waited in a comfortable hotel for about two weeks for the arrival of the *"Salamis"*. I never had such a good time in my life; nothing to do but eat good meals and go to the beach for afternoon swims, with ideal weather all the time. Weir's bought the *"Salamis"* from the Aberdeen Line and I think I mentioned already that I was offered the 4th mate's job in her in Melbourne after I got my 2nd mate's ticket there in 1907. Captain Howie who left us in Galveston at the outbreak of war was Marine Superintendent in Durban, so we were old friends. After I joined the ship and we began loading, he told me that every voyage a consignment, consisting of 500 1-cwt bags of a valuable mineral, which was mixed with tin in Malaya, was placed and counted aboard the ship by himself as it was worth £20 a bag, but every voyage it was short landed in Singapore and he could not understand how or where the shortage occurred. Always the shortage was valued in Singapore at about £400 and the ship had to pay this amount. Would I keep a special eye on the whole thing? When it was loaded Captain Howie himself counted the 500 bags and I knew they were aboard, so I was determined to catch the thieves in Singapore. When the lighter arrived, I put on as tally men the 3rd mate and an apprentice; besides them there was a Chinaman to do the tallying for the ship and another Chinaman by the receiving merchant and, of course, I was myself keeping an eye on the business. I put the 2nd mate in the lighter to see that the bags were put in a row aboard the lighter so that they could be easily counted. When the last slings of bags were landed in the lighter the two Chinese announced that we were 20 bags short landed. The 3rd mate and the young apprentice confirmed the figure. This left me very angry so I refused to allow the lighter to leave the side of the ship till every bag was counted, which was very easy through the way in which they were loaded in the lighter. Just then the Captain came on board, also the agent. The Captain said, 'Heave up and we shall be off.'

I said, 'No. We shall first count all the bags in the lighter, even if we stay here all night.'

Anyway, I took both tallymen and the 2nd mate with me and we all counted the bags and, lo and behold the Chinese tallymen had to admit defeat and, as the ship's agent was an observer of what was happening, I got a receipt for the whole quantity and that was the end of the robbery.

On the return journey to South Africa, the agent informed me that they found out how the shortages happened. A Chinese sampan met the lighter and took 20 bags off it before it reached the shore. The ship got the blame, but the tallymen got a share of the loot.

Before I left London Captain MacBride, our Marine Superintendent, had told me that he knew, sitting at his desk in London, that the ship was not being stowed properly in Hong Kong, for she was not carrying the cargo for the space available in her. He was Superintendent in Hong Kong before coming to London. Here was another problem I had to solve and I was determined to get to the bottom of it. We took the usual cargo, mostly cases of silk in Japanese ports, and I knew when we got to Hong Kong, where the bulk of the cargo came aboard, that I had space to spare. I was up and down the holds during loading and saw to it that not one corner of the ship was empty. When we finished loading all the cargo that was booked by the office, the Manager came aboard to make certain we had available the space for 500 tons which he had booked for Singapore. He was very surprised when I told him that there was space left for 1,100 tons.

'Impossible!' he said, as we had booked the same as the previous voyages.

'Well,' said I, 'it will only take a few minutes to measure it.'

'I'll take your word for it,' he said.

So he immediately left the ship and booked further cargo at Singapore which was easy enough as there was a real shortage of tonnage in the world through the Germans sinking tonnage on a large scale.

The Captain of the *"Salamis"* was a very easy-going man and took very little interest in the working of the ship. The shipping merchants of Singapore sent more cargo alongside than they were asked to, so finally I filled every corner in the ship including some space in the bunkers and also put a small quantity on the deck aft. It was merely a few bundles of rattans. Freights were very high and probably I was a bit ambitious to make as much money as possible for the owners. All went well till we got to Mauritius and after the pilot came on board. The wind was blowing out of the harbour and we had to go into the harbour stern first. I was on the forecastle head, the place where the Chief Mate is always on duty, when leaving or entering port, and I had ample opportunity to watch the handling of the ship. The pilot and, I suppose, the Captain hesitated to go full speed astern against the wind and ordered the mooring rope to be made fast to the buoy too soon. The result was that the wind got the ship before the mooring boat got to the buoy, and, as the engines could not be put astern in case the mooring line fouled the propeller, our ship drifted down on another ship but did not do any damage. Eventually she got straightened up and we made fast to the buoy.

The Captain got furious. He met me coming off the forecastle head and accused me of the bad handling of the ship through putting cargo on deck, which, by the way was not obstructing the mooring line or the machinery heaving it in. I got very angry and said that what happened was due entirely to the incompetence of the men on the bridge, which was the truth. That made him more furious and he said he would report me to the London office.

'Go ahead,' I said, 'and if you tell the truth, I will not get blamed.'

With that we parted. I was still angry later as I was going down into one of the bunker 'tweendecks to see about some cargo that was to be landed. I had a couple of apprentices there to watch things and began instructing them and was walking backwards when all of a sudden they both shouted, 'Look out, Sir!'

But it was too late; I fell into the lower-hold, probably 12 feet or more, but luckily landed on some loose coal. I was shaken up and little bits of coal got into my skin in the face. I got to my room and lay down and both the doctor and the Captain pronounced no bones broken. The old Captain was very sympathetic. He was a nice man really, but his only concern was the passengers. We carried only 12 Europeans, but about 100 Chinese under the bridge deck. They were really deck passengers.

At this stage I had better tell a story the purser told me. He was also the wireless operator. On the voyage before I joined the ship, when the ship was all ready to sail for the Far East via Mauritius, the Captain received a cable from London to hold back the ship for a day or two as the Governor of Mauritius was travelling on one of the Castle Liners as far as Durban and the best cabin was to be reserved for him. Within 36 hours he was aboard with his staff and the ship sailed and, of course, the Captain was very happy to have the Governor aboard. He was very much inclined to kow-tow to men like the Governor or any high official. The ship was bumping into a head wind and, as she was practically light, she was losing speed and the delay in getting into Mauritius was very irritating to the Governor; he was inclined to snap at everyone, including the Captain. Colonial governors in those days considered themselves very important.

The ship arrived in port about 30 hours or more late. The mate got the deck washed down and put out the accommodation ladder and cleaned it. The ladder was very old, a self-adjusting type, and through old age the bearing on the adjusting apparatus were worn down so that the steps were very rickety and difficult to walk on unless you were accustomed to them. What the mate should have done really was to put sand on the steps instead of water. After breakfast the Governor appeared on deck, dressed up in his gold braid cocked hat and his sword. He surveyed the whole place with his monocle. The harbour was crowded with boats with men and women in them all dressed up and the boats beflagged and everyone waving to the Governor. He walked down the accommodation ladder and had only gone a few steps when the heel of his shoe slipped on the rickety steps. He dropped on his bottom on the ladder and slithered down the steps with his sword dangling after him till he landed on the bottom platform with his feet in the water. He managed to pull himself together and jumped into his big barge which awaited him. I presume nobody laughed.

When the Chinamen became old or feeble they all decided to go back home. On that voyage one of them died, but his friends aboard were so intent on getting him to China that they had hidden his body under the fresh water tank and there was an awful row, with the mate threatening all sorts of things at which the Chinese passengers were horrified. The mate was from the east coast of Scotland and was very superstitious and after I relieved him in the *"Salamis"*, he joined one the firm's other ships in London. In a gale she broke adrift in the dock and he swore that there were bad spirits aboard her and left the next day.

To get back to my own job, I have explained my fall into the lower hold. I was up and about the next morning as usual and, as Captain Howie in Durban had told me that one of the worst ports for pilfering was Port Louis, Mauritius, especially of silk, I had to be on my guard all the time we were there. It was usual to have claims of about £400 every voyage. I knew I did not lose much there. When we got back from Cape Town and arrived in Durban for the next voyage to Japan, Captain Howie had all the claims for my first voyage. They amounted to £39, so I was well pleased with all my efforts.

Nothing much happened on the voyage up till we reached Hong Kong. A police launch stopped us as the pilot came aboard and several policemen came on board and told me that about £60,000 worth of opium was on board and the ship might be delayed for hours before getting to the buoys to be moored. Sure enough, opium was discovered on board to the tune of £30,000. We had several hundred deck passengers aboard from Singapore and, of course, some from Mauritius. There was a gang of men in the opium deal and someone said that one who was not satisfied with his part of the loot had informed the police. When all the passengers and crew were questioned, none of them knew about the opium. The opium was confiscated, but none of the gang of men responsible was caught, so whoever got it aboard would plan carefully so that his next haul would not be confiscated. The smugglers had been at the game for years and no doubt several hauls of opium were taken into Hong Kong without being detected.

As usual we went as far as Yokohama to load our usual cargo of silk, etc, for South Africa, and on our way back we loaded more cargo at Kobe. There we took on board a Japanese pilot to take us as far as Moji; in other words, he was piloting us through the Inland Sea of Japan. At about 3.30am I heard a great commotion on deck which woke me up and just then the 2nd mate rushed in to say that we had run into a schooner and broken her in two. I, of course, rushed on deck and got a boat's crew with myself in charge into the water. This was a wooden schooner, loaded with coal and our ship, which was travelling at thirteen knots, had gone right through her. One half drifted away to starboard and the other half to port. The night was quite dark but calm, so I steered my boat in the darkness to the part of the schooner from which I could hear shouting and yelling arising. It was not long before I reached the fore half of the schooner and aboard were a man and a woman. Thinking they were pinned between the wreckage, I naturally jumped aboard to try and get them extricated as the woman was still shrieking. Whichever part of the wreck I stepped on it gave way and I found myself up to the neck in water. However, I soon caught a solid bit of wood and pulled myself up and found the man and woman both well and unhurt. The woman who, I discovered afterwards, was the man's wife was really yelling at the man and pointing at the entrance of their cabin. By this time daylight had come. The man was not saying a word, but was willing to come aboard my lifeboat and abandon the wreck, but the woman flatly refused. I asked one of my Chinese crew if he could interpret, as he said he had a smattering of Japanese, but all he could extract from the woman was that there was something in the cabin which was full of water that she wanted and was bullying her husband to go down into the water and fetch it, but he sat down and would not answer her. In the end I tried to make as clear as possible to her that I would leave her on the wreck but in a few hours it would drift ashore near Hiroshima. Just them she herself dived into the cabin full of water and in a minute was up again holding thirty yen in her hand, equal in those days to about £1.10s. I admired her pluck and her old man sulked even more. Evidently the schooner belonged to themselves and the two of them ran it. When we hit them right amidships, the cargo of coal dropped to the bottom of the sea, but both ends of the schooner, being wooden, floated.

After I got on board we proceeded on our way to Moji where we were taking bunkers aboard. The Captain and the pilot had to go to a Marine Court to give evidence about the cause of the collision. It was proven that the schooner was not showing any lights so her Captain was entirely to blame, but as the schooner was his only asset it was decided that if the Captain of our ship paid him £30, there would be no further trouble and he could sail for Hong Kong as arranged. The Captain was very pleased to do so and everyone was happy, but the happiest of the crowd was the silent husband and his mate and, as she was so keen on saving £1.10s., I hope she got a little of the £30.

While loading in Hong Kong, I was looking over the rail on the saloon deck one afternoon and my attention was drawn to a sampan lying at our gangway. This sampan, like thousands of others, was the home of a family. This particular one was hired by the ship for sending and receiving messages and passengers from the shore and had aboard Father, Mother, three children and a cat. The sampan was their only home and their only shelter in it was a canopy under which they all slept and ate. I forget the amount we paid for the hire of this sampan but it was very small. As I mentioned already, while looking over the rail, I noticed that the crawling baby fell overboard and was yelling his head off. I, of course, immediately called to his Mother who was busy cooking, but she did not seem very concerned and kept on with her work. At last she suddenly stopped and looked over the rail of the sampan, picked the child up and dropped him on the floor of the sampan. It was then I noticed that the baby had a safety belt on. This was an inflated bladder of some small animal, firmly tied around the child's shoulders. She (the Mother) knew very well that the child was quite safe in the water, hence her lack of concern regarding him.

CHAPTER ELEVEN

We went on our way back to South Africa and all went well except that a lighter with hundreds of Chinese crackers aboard went on fire alongside the ship in Mauritius. The 3rd mate woke up first, or else he was on duty at the time. He rushed to my room and when I got up there were Chinese crackers popping away in all directions. Luckily the wind was in the right direction and took the lighter with it on to a sand bank after the ropes were let go.

I said to the 3rd mate, 'Where did you go when I was letting go the lighter's ropes?'

'Well,' he said, 'you know, I bought a new uniform suit in Hong Kong and I jumped into my room to put it on in case the ship went on fire.'

There was a lot to be said for this point of view in a man who had not much money and had to spend a good part of it on his new uniform. We had peace and quiet after that and did our usual round to the Cape.

On the way back to China and Japan we had the usual number of saloon passengers (12) and a large number of Chinese deck passengers. In the saloon there was a woman with children from Reunion and somehow or other the children were making a mess in the saloon's bathroom and lavatory. One morning at breakfast the Captain complained to the Chinese Chief Steward that neither the lavatory nor the bathroom was very clean.

'Sir,' he said. 'How can I keep the place clean when all the children sh.. sh.. sh.. sh.. all the time there?'

The Captain was very unwise to mention such a delicate subject at the breakfast table.

Large numbers of deck passengers boarded the ship at Singapore and very likely some of them were smugglers; if so they were not found out.

As the northeast monsoons were blowing very hard after leaving Singapore the Captain decided to set a course for Cape Padran, Indo-China, as he thought he would get better weather on that course. One evening at about 6.30pm I took star observations and fixed the position on the chart and told the Captain that the ship was 30 miles off course and if he did not alter the present course, he would not sight Cape Padran lighthouse as he expected since he would be outside the range of it. He turned to me and asked me how I knew and I said I had worked out star observations and put the position on the chart and that it must be right as I had cross-checked it with two stars.

He said, 'These new-fangled ideas about stars have no meaning and I don't believe in them.'

I went to bed and to sleep. Just about midnight I was woken up by being thrown out of bed and before I could get to my feet, the 3rd mate was in my room shouting at me to be on deck at once as the old Captain was going to pile the ship on the shore. I lost no time in getting on to the bridge and when I got there the old Captain had left the bridge and was down in the saloon deck consoling the Reunion woman and her children who had run out of their cabin shouting and weeping.

What really happened was that the Captain thought he struck Cape Padran and that the light was obscured by haze, so he put the helm hard 'a port to get away from it. Actually he struck a 2½ fathom reef patch about 40 miles to the east of Cape Padran and when he put the helm hard over to get away from the land, right in front of him was a pillar of rock about 100 feet high or more and that was what the 3rd mate saw when he came rushing into my room. Luckily, through the swing of the helm the ship cleared the pillar of rock and I got her on her course as I had enough sense and knowledge to know where the ship actually was.

All the passengers, both from the saloon and the deck, were very perturbed and were out on deck although it was very dark, for most of them had wakened up when the ship passed over the 18 feet reef and, naturally, were all questioning the Captain who was still on the saloon deck soothing the female passengers. He kept on telling them that it was alright and that the ship hit a sunken wreck and she was alright and no damage done. I assured myself before going back to bed that she was not taking any water in by sending the carpenter to sound all the holds.

The Captain wrote to the owners from Hong Kong to say that the ship hit a sunken wreck, but it would be advisable to dry dock her on our arrival at Kobe. This was done and when the ship was in dry dock, I noticed that the edges of the plates in the bottom of the ship had a large amount of coral stuck to them, so I knew that the ship had gathered them as she scraped along the top of the reef. It was lucky for us that the ship was not drawing more than 19 feet when we passed the reef, otherwise she would have stuck on it for good. Grinding over the reef at full speed of 13 knots certainly dented several plates between the frames, but did not do any permanent damage.

While we were loading this voyage in Yokohama we encountered one of the worst typhoons I had ever experienced. Although lots of small craft were lost and damaged, none of the big ships in the harbour tied to the buoys suffered any damage. I never went ashore in Yokohama, but this last voyage I nearly did as I noticed in one of the local English papers that there was a Mrs. Murchison staying in one of the big hotels. I, however, did not pluck up the courage to call on her. My feeling was that she was a grand lady with pots of money and that she would not want to see a mere chief officer of a ship. Ever since then I have been sorry I did not see her for, looking back on it, I am sure a Murchison man or woman would have been pleased to meet one of their own clan, especially in a foreign country.

We loaded the usual cargo and called at the usual ports, but nothing of importance occurred and no excitement as far as I remember happened till we reached Cape Town. There we were told that the ship was taken over to transport troops to East Africa and large parts of the ship were gutted and bunks and hammocks were fitted to receive troops.

We were for the best part of three weeks in Cape Town, fitting out the ship to carry over 1,000 men and about 40 to 50 officers and sergeants. These were grand days for us with nothing much to do but the usual routine of the ship. At last the day of embarkation arrived and the troops, 500 of them, came on board and we sailed for Durban to pick up the balance of about 500. Going round the Cape of Good Hope it came on to blow from the south east, a head gale really, but we were pretty light, in fact we had to put some stone ballast in two holds as the ship had no water ballast tanks. The ship was really going nicely against the gale and was shipping no water at all. Just as

I was coming off watch at 8pm the Chief Engineer came on to the bridge and said that he would have to stop the ship for about an hour.

Both the Captain and I said, 'Well, she will roll the masts out of her when she falls into the trough of these heavy seas.'

This was really figuratively speaking.

'Nevertheless, we shall have to stop her to get some repairs carried out.'

The night was fairly warm although the wind was so high, so most of the troops took their hammocks on deck and were mainly sleeping on the saloon deck. Most of them were seasick.

The officer commanding troops had the men sleeping in rows on the saloon deck and space was left for people walking along the deck without disturbing the soldiers. As I was leaving the bridge and handing over to the 3rd mate at about 8.15pm, the ship stopped and fell into the trough of the heavy seas. I rushed along the deck and jumped into the wireless room which was in the after deck and managed to prop myself in a chair when the ship took a heavy lurch to windward and all the troops were flung against the rail; some of them indeed went feet first through the rail, but were too big to fall overboard. Suddenly, the ship took a lurch to leeward and pandemonium ruled on deck.

I heard one soldier say to another, 'Watch her this time, Bob, she is sure going to coup.'

She really did roll and some of the officers tried to get the soldiers below, but being below would not help them, unless they got their hammocks tied up securely. Within an hour we got the ship on her course and things improved. One or two of the lifeboats were damaged slightly, but some of the other ships in the convoy were badly damaged as they were loaded deeply down to their marks.

We were only a couple of days in Durban when we got away for East Africa. The first day at sea we had boat drill. I remember one of the old soldiers telling a crowd of young ones after everyone was allotted to a boat or raft that he had been on seven blinking troopships since the war began and in everyone of them he was placed on a raft and, 'what hope has anyone on a bloody raft, I tell you, just look at it and imagine yourself on the wide ocean on it!'

Once we got on the east coast they kept us there, ferrying troops from one port to another, but some way or other our military never got near the Germans with their African troops.

A troopship arrived from the west coast of Africa with a whole regiment of West Africans and the mate told me that when the troopship was approaching Cape Town, the West African troops were very interested in the blaze of lights and one man said to another that he had never seen such a big bush fire in his life.

We were kept busy and had little rest. One of the German men-of-war hid herself up the Rufiji river and one of our men-of-war came out after her from bombarding the coast of Belgium. She was a flat bottom ship with very heavy guns aboard called the *"Severn"*. She was no time in subduing the small German cruiser and we took all the prisoners from her to Dar-es-Salaam, but most of the crew escaped to join Von Lettow, the German General.

I remember the officers and men we had and how in the early morning I had to go down to the troop deck where I saw our soldiers who were guarding the German prisoners sound asleep and their rifles lying alongside them. Of course, the Germans were also sound asleep, but it has often occurred to me that if the German sailors with their officers aboard had had any gumption they would have got our soldiers' rifles and attacked and captured the ship. None of our crew or officers were armed. Anyway, the Germans were safely landed in Dar-es-Salaam.

On another voyage down the coast, we put into Port Amelia in Portuguese East Africa for prisoners for Dar-es-Salaam. The military police came aboard with a prisoner and he was put in the cells right away. I asked them why he was deserving of such treatment and they told me that he was caught with the thigh of a woman, eating it, after he had shot her, and he was being sent to Dar-es-Salaam to be court martialled. He was a very small man but sturdy, and the cells were in the orlop deck. The beams holding the deck above were wide apart and very deep, the result being that there was quite a space between the beams, which was never closed up, for nobody ever thought a man could get out. However, our cannibal escaped during the night and swam ashore, but I suppose he hadn't a clue how to get out of the town for the military officer in charge told me later that he was caught and shot at dawn. I suppose he thought there was no harm in what he did and that his tribe were always cannibals.

Another coast voyage we went on was to Mombasa to embark porters for Lindi, a port further south. These porters were from near Lake Victoria and were recruited there and a British missionary was put in charge of them. When they boarded our ship they were practically naked, but they were handed khaki trousers and a few other things like bush shirts and a blanket. We landed in a couple of days at Lindi and the first night ashore when they lighted a fire to cook their evening meal, they placed a few mills bombs round to keep the pot steady. So, of course, the bombs burst and several of them were killed. Whenever a regiment was on the march, 1,000 porters had to trail after them to carry ammunition and other stores. That was war in the bush.

After discharging more stores, we were going back to Dar-es-Salaam and, when heaving the anchor in, we saw a launch with a few men in it towing a small craft after it; the men were waving frantically to us. The Captain shouted to me to avast heaving in case these people in the launch had an urgent message for us. Anyway, I walked back to the accommodation ladder to receive them and two or three Army officers came on board and I was quite cordial to them and said I would now go and heave the anchor up.

'No! No! No! Chief,' they muttered. 'We have a bit of ivory in the boat astern. Please allow us to take it on board.'

At this I got agitated and told them in no uncertain manner that there was a war on and every minute wasted was criminal. I further told them what I thought of military officers carrying ivory about as luggage, but by this time their luggage and ivory were aboard. One of them said they were for a long time in the bush and picked the ivory up there and were taking it to India. As the three officers were dressed in shorts and bush shirts, I did not notice the pips on their shoulders, but later on I noticed that one of them was a brigadier and, besides, was a V.C. Perhaps he saw the justice of my remarks about the ivory for he never mentioned it and was very cordial to me when he left us the next day.

When we were in Mombasa for further troops, who should come aboard but my own brother Murdo. He had been a Captain in the Cameron Highlanders in France and had been badly wounded there, and when he recovered in about six months he was seconded to an East African Regiment as, presumably, he would not be fit enough to proceed to France for a long period. He was the most senior military officer on board so was, in accordance with Army rules, the officer commanding troops. (Later on we had a permanent officer commanding troops on board.)

Many an argument my brother and I had, especially after inspection. His adjutant was very often in the arguments, but we never really had a row. But on one occasion I was very upset when they ordered one of the soldiers to receive 30 lashes with a strap made of hide. I said it was criminal and uncivilised to administer punishment in that fashion, but they always fell back on the African Army code.

While Murdo and his adjutant were staying in a hotel in Mombasa their money was stolen and when they came on board they were "stony broke". They asked if they could sign my name in the bar book, which I permitted them to do. Army officers always had to pay cash for their drinks. I was a strict teetotaller in those days so my bill at the bar did not amount to much although I was quite generous with drinks to my friends. Drinks were cheap anyway, a bottle of whisky cost 2/. However, when my brother and his friend left us (they were three weeks aboard), I was presented with a huge bill of about £14, for drinks at the end of the month. I protested to the steward, but he said that my brother and adjutant and their friends had all their drinks free.

About this time my cousin Jessie Murchison arrived in Dar-es-Salaam. She was my father's brother John's daughter and was a nurse with the Army in Gallipoli, so through her I got to know many of the nurses in the hospital in Dar-es-Salaam. She and a few more were sent down to Lindi, a real bush town. They lived in tents. Shortly after they arrived they told me that one night they heard lions roaring outside their tent. Jessie told me she got C.B. while in the Army, the first woman who was ever confined to barracks, up till 1917 anyway. Actually, she was in the right, but the major in charge was a great friend of the Matron and, of course, took her side in the quarrel.

* * *

I saw Jessie recently now in 1962 she is 87 and living in Glasgow.

* * *

During one of her trips to South Africa from East Africa in 1917 the hospital ship she was in called at Durban. There were two ships berthed alongside her ship - one was the *"Huntcliff"* and our cousin, K. MacDonald, was Captain of her. The ship outside was a Hall steamer of which my brother Roderick was mate. That is how war brought people together. My brother, Murdo, went up country, but he did not stay long in East Africa as he was called home to continue his medical studies, but by the time he got home via Mauritius and Bombay the war was nearly over.

Von Lettow, the German General, kept our army on the move all the time and after losing all trace of his whereabouts for a long while, he was reported to be active on the borders of Portuguese territory, so we got orders to take troops and stores from East African ports to Beira. We proceeded to Kilwa and Lindi with all speed and the ship was so full of African troops that the doctor came to me in great haste to report that there was no further space in the troop deck, so what was to be done? Further craft, full of troops, were meantime leaving the shore.

I said, 'When the main deck is full, then put them round the funnel.'

We mostly picked up military stores in Lindi and in the late evening we finished and sailed at 8pm. As I was very tired, I went to bed after heaving up anchor, etc.

At midnight the second mate rushed into my cabin to say that we were on a coral reef. I went out to the bridge and the Captain said the same thing, but we could not see anything. It was a fearfully dark night and by now the ship was bumping on the coral, so I sent the carpenter to sound the bilges. He reported back no water, which was a relief. We sent for the wireless operator to report our plight. Meantime, the bumping stopped and I knew we must have gone ashore on the top of high water; although we tried by giving the engines full power astern, the old ship refused to budge.

Meanwhile the Captain came to me and said he had dysentery and was going to bed. Just then the wireless operator came up to tell us that the cruiser *"Talbot"* had told us to shut up and not to use our wireless. I was really afraid that we might be on the edge of the reef and, when the tide left us high and dry, the ship might slip off and cause serious damage, although by the sounding around the ship it was unlikely. Anyway, I said to the wireless operator to send an S.O.S. which he did and to say that we had over 2,000 troops aboard. No sooner had he sent the message off than the *"Talbot"* sent a message that all ships were to listen to the S.O.S. All ships did and within an hour there were nearly half a dozen ships rushing towards us.

I was really sorry for the Captain. He was really a very decent man, but did not take the navigation of his ship very seriously. This time we had the General and all his staff aboard - Van Deventer or just Deventer was his name. The Captain was anxious to please and make a quick passage to Beira. The current had been very strong going into Lindi harbour when we left, but he made no allowance for that. He just sailed for about an hour out in an ENE direction and then altered the course to a south-easterly direction to pass Delgado Point, but in order to cut off a mile or two, he decided to pass between a reef and the shore. This reef is only 6 or 7 miles off the coast and on a dark night, with no lights to guide him, it was a very risky thing to do.

There was nothing we could do but hang around and await daylight. All the soldiers and most of the crew were asleep. They never heard the ship going ashore. Indeed some of the officers were playing bridge till the early hours of the morning.

I was very much amused by a story one of the officers told me. They were playing bridge in their cabin and were very late going to bed.

When the breakfast gong went one of them jumped out of bed and exclaimed in astonishment, 'Boys, we're in the bush and no sight of the sea!'

'Go on, old chap. You had too much to drink last night,' shouted the other three officers. 'Yes,' shouted the three again who were still in their bunks. 'They are putting wheels on the ship and we are going to chase Von Lettow across Africa instead of sailing to Beira.'

The officer that saw that we were in the bush was quite right for the ship had gone ashore on the mainland and not on the reef six miles off the shore. We were a long way out of our course and, furthermore, she went ashore at high water and we were almost into the bushes, and when the officer mentioned above looked out of the port hole, the tide was out which left the ship high and dry.

I stayed on deck all night and, when dawn arrived, I saw that the ship was in no danger, so I ordered a lot of heavy equipment to be thrown overboard from the forward hold. Shortly after daylight the ships coming to our assistance were coming into sight, including the H.M.S. *"Talbot"* and also the heavy armed monitor H.M.S. *"Severn"*, which was a shallow draft ship as I have mentioned already. The Captain of the *"Severn"* came aboard to offer his assistance. If I remember rightly his name was Jones. He was really a Lt. Commander R.N., but acting Captain.

Our Captain was still in bed, so Captain Jones and I agreed to get the troops off the ship as soon as possible. I launched all our lifeboats and I took the port side of our ship and he the starboard side with our 2nd officer in charge with him. Orders were given to all units to get their equipment ready and half were ordered to step to port and half to the starboard side with fatigue parties to help. The disembarking got started about lunch time and by 5pm we had all troops off the ship. Commander Jones came to me to congratulate me on finishing first and said that he was good at swearing but that I must be better than he for, otherwise, how could I get all those native troops off the ship so quickly?

After the troops were off the ship, I felt happier and we had a quieter night and all the crew had a good rest. The ship bumped a lot with the ground swell coming in at high water, but we could not get her to budge, so next morning we dumped more cargo and the *"Talbot"* passed us a line to which we attached our own heavier wires. At high water the H.M.S. *"Talbot"* started to try to pull our ship off with our engines going full speed astern. Still we could not budge. By this time the Captain was out of bed and able to take some nourishment. The Chinese bosun came to me and said that in China the night tides were sometimes higher than the day tides and I said to him that in the Highlands of Scotland it is also so. By this time we had lightened the ship from the forward end a good deal and threw some store ballast we had in No. 1 lower hold overboard. At about 1am we went up on the bridge, including the Captain as he was feeling better. We put the engines full speed astern and, lo and behold, the ship floated away quite easily; so we proceeded on our way to Beira to discharge vehicles and other military equipment still on board. The ship was making no water in spite of the pounding she got on the coral beach.

We began to discharge large ambulances and lorries immediately on our arrival in Beira into lighters and at 5pm, the last of the lighters left us for the shore.

We had finished dinner at about 7.15pm when we heard a terrific explosion which shook the ship from end to end. I rushed out on deck, thinking the fore part of the ship had been blown off but as far as I could see, the ship was not hit or damaged at all. I however, could see from the ship that there was some commotion around the lighters' wharf and we learnt afterwards that the explosion occurred aboard one of the lighters which had left our ship about two hours before. It appeared that some spy or other had placed bombs in the lighter or lighters. The only damage caused was around the lighters' wharf, but a large number of windows were shattered in the town. Luckily the bomb went off after all work along the wharves had ceased. Beira, being a Portuguese territory, a hunt for spies began the next day, but none was caught; but we heard that all the Greek grocers in Beira were on the way out into other territories the next morning, for they had assured themselves that they, or some of them, would be blamed as the Portuguese had not much love for them. Strange as it may sound, most of the grocery businesses all the way down the river Nile and in East Africa right down to Beira were in Greek hands. The general opinion is that as these territories were opened up, the Greeks followed with their usual astute business methods. Some of them were probably Egyptian Greeks who were never in Greece. We never heard if they found the culprits who caused the explosion as we sailed back for Dar-es-Salaam. In the harbour was H.M.S. *"Talbot"*, so the next day she hoisted a signal to say that all the officers and the Captain of the *"Salamis"* were to come aboard at 11am. Ten minutes later another signal was hoisted in the man-of-war to say that the Captain, 2nd and 3rd officers of the *"Salamis"* were to appear aboard, but not the Chief Officer, so I was quite pleased to be out of it. There was a Court of Enquiry aboard and the Captain and 2nd officer were severely reprimanded for careless navigation, etc. on board the *"Salamis"*, but I think the 3rd mate got off. Nothing else was done about it and my name was not mentioned at the enquiry.

Next day we got orders to proceed to Cape Town, South Africa, to refit and dry dock. The ship was due for dry docking anyway and we all had a good time in Cape Town for about three weeks. We got into a terrible gale off Port Elizabeth and on our starboard bow was another transport ship, the *"City of Athens"*. We lost sight of her in the gale for we could not see very well or far on account of the spindrift rising off the sea through the gale. She appeared to be making much worse weather of the gale than we did, as she was deeply loaded and we were half light and rode the gale without shipping water.

In due course the gale abated and we arrived in Cape Town, but there was no sign of the *"City of Athens"*. She, however, arrived later on and was damaged, though not severely. While we were in Cape Town the *"Cutty Sark"*, the old tea clipper, arrived there very badly damaged and partly dismasted. She was under Portuguese ownership and was rigged as a barque, but nevertheless appeared a beautiful ship. I saw her in dry dock and admired her beautiful lines. No wonder she sailed well, especially in her days of glory! She got re-rigged in Cape Town and was a long time getting her spars, sails and damaged hull fully repaired. Her whole cargo was discharged and reloaded in Cape Town and must have cost the insurance a tidy sum.

After our three weeks in Cape Town, which we enjoyed, as previously mentioned, we loaded some cargo and proceeded to Durban where we loaded more stores for the military in East Africa. I might have mentioned this already, but on our arrival at Dar-es-Salaam the stevedores were told that all the officers' stores, whisky, brandy and all kinds of wine were to be discharged at once. The stores by the way mostly consisted of booze for all the officer's messes in town and up country and as we had a small company of the Dublin Fusiliers aboard for disembarkation at Mombasa, they were told to form a fatigue party to get all stores off the ship. Work went on till early morning and all stores were sent ashore in the lighters. As we were leaving early in the morning for Mombasa, I was up at daylight and went to the forecastle head to get the cable off the buoy.

I was astonished to see a number of the Fusiliers lying anyhow on the forecastle head, so I shouted to them, 'Come on now, lads, you must get away from here,' as we had to unship the cable from the buoy and put a shiprope on it, but there was no response from the men, so I started shaking them up, but still no movement out of them.

'Good Lord,' I said to myself. 'These boys are all dead!'

So I sent for the doctor right away. He was there in a few minutes, rubbing his eyes and examining the men.

'No, Chief,' he said (a quietly spoken man). 'They're not dead; they are just dead drunk.'

'Well,' said I. 'I have seen in my days and travels many a drunk sailor, but never so bad as these men.'

It then occurred to me that they were the fatigue party who helped to discharge the officers' messes booze.

We were kept on the coast, shifting troops and stores and getting no newspapers except those from home, which were generally two or three months old. There was a local paper in Mombasa, but we did not reach as far north except on special occasions. I used to go ashore now and again in Dar-es-Salaam to look at the posted news put outside Military Headquarters, and by the summer of 1918, I thought the Bulgarians were going to cave in and, sure enough, by the autumn they were breaking up. But the German General, Von Lettow, gave no word of giving in and the British Army kept on chasing him. As late as the autumn of 1918 we were in Mombasa embarking porters for Mozambique. What a queer crowd they looked! About 1,000 of them came on board with nothing on but a blanket they had got from the British Army.

They had never seen the sea before and when we got outside Mombasa harbour and the ship began pitching into the south west monsoon, it was fascinating to watch them. They were on their knees - not to pray, but presumably they were frightened to stand in case they fell. An English missionary was in charge of them with the rank of Captain. I always thought how silly it was, bringing all these people from the bush to fight Germans and the Germans gathering a like number from the bush to fight the British, but that is how the war was fought in East Africa.

Von Lettow was never caught, nor his army completely beaten and when the Armistice was signed in Europe, officers had to try and reach Von Lettow with white flags to inform him that the war was over. He was completely out of touch with what was going on in Europe.

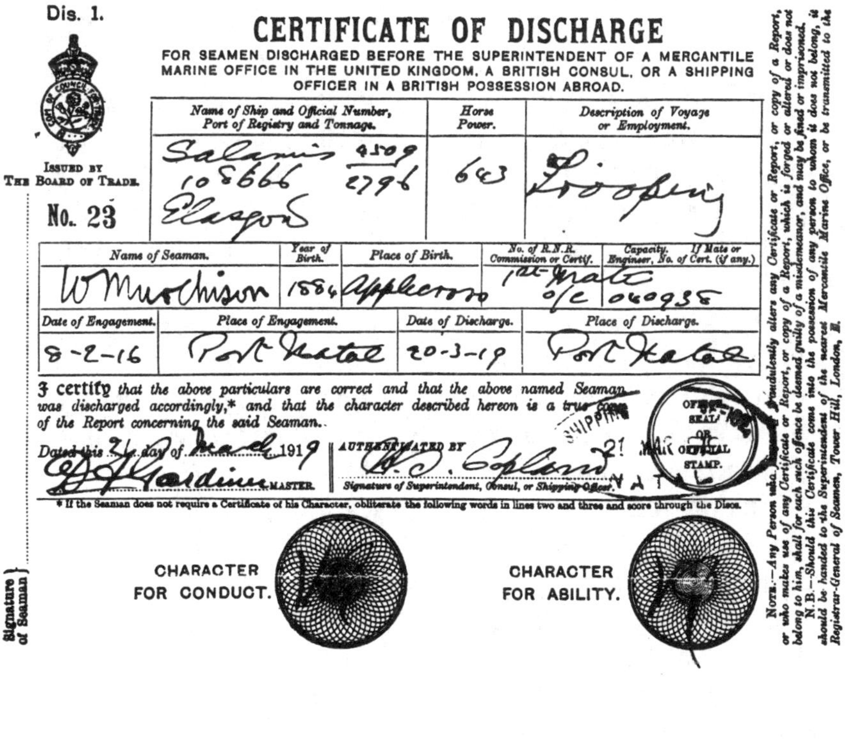

Dis. 1.

ISSUED BY THE BOARD OF TRADE.

No. 23

CERTIFICATE OF DISCHARGE

FOR SEAMEN DISCHARGED BEFORE THE SUPERINTENDENT OF A MERCANTILE MARINE OFFICE IN THE UNITED KINGDOM, A BRITISH CONSUL, OR A SHIPPING OFFICER IN A BRITISH POSSESSION ABROAD.

Name of Ship and Official Number, Port of Registry and Tonnage.	*Horse Power.*	*Description of Voyage or Employment.*
Salamis 4509 105666 2796 Glasgow	643	Trooping

Name of Seaman.	*Year of Birth.*	*Place of Birth.*	*No. of R.N.R. Commission or Certif.*	*Capacity. If Mate or Engineer, No. of Cert. (if any.)*
W Murchison	1884	Applecross		1st Mate O/C 060935

Date of Engagement.	*Place of Engagement.*	*Date of Discharge.*	*Place of Discharge.*
8-2-16	Port Natal	20-3-19	Port Natal

I certify *that the above particulars are correct and that the above named Seaman was discharged accordingly,* and that the character described hereon is a true copy of the Report concerning the said Seaman.*

Dated this 24 *day of* March 1919 — MASTER.

AUTHENTICATED BY — *Signature of Superintendent, Consul, or Shipping Officer.*

OFFICIAL SEAL OR OFFICIAL STAMP.

* If the Seaman does not require a Certificate of his Character, obliterate the following words in lines two and three and score through the Discs.

CHARACTER FOR CONDUCT.

CHARACTER FOR ABILITY.

Signature of Seaman.

NOTE.—Any Person who fraudulently alters any Certificate or Report, or copy of a Report, or who makes use of any Certificate or Report, or copy of a Report, which is forged or altered or does not belong to him, shall for each such offence be deemed guilty of a misdemeanor, and may be fined or imprisoned.

N.B.—Should this Certificate come into the possession of any person to whom it does not belong, it should be handed to the Superintendent of the nearest Mercantile Marine Office, or be transmitted to the Registrar-General of Shipping and Seamen, Tower Hill, London, E.

CHAPTER TWELVE

We were in Mozambique when the Armistice came, so we beflagged the ship for the occasion. Now our task was to take all the troops back to their original destinations, so we went a few times to Mombasa before we got orders to carry troops from East Africa to Durban to connect with empty troopships from Australia - homewards. This job was very much to our liking.

Some of us took the bad flu that was so prevalent all over the world at that time. I got it, but was only a few days in bed. In fact it was not too bad at all on our ship, but one hospital ship, the *"Gloucester Castle"*, had to stay in port for several days as there wasn't a fit man aboard to get her to sea, at least not enough officers or engineers fit enough to keep watch at sea.

We began embarking troops for Durban for British troops were in charge of all the bases in East Africa and everyone was anxious to be out of it and get home. We called after leaving Dar-es-Salaam to lift launches and officers and men from a little port called Port Amelia in Portuguese East Africa, and by 5pm everything was ready except to get two launches aboard. We had just hauled up the heavier of the launches a few inches from the water when a shackle in the topping lift of the derrick gave way and down came the derrick and smashed a temporary house on deck, and the launch went back into the water. Two officers whom I did not know said quite loudly,

'Now we shall be here for another day and probably lose our connection for England.'

Meantime I sent some sailors aloft to renew the shackle and I had the derrick and the launch aboard within half an hour and we sailed at the stated time.

One voyage to Durban and back was just like another. We brought troops down and took civilians back. Most of them were anxious to get home to Nairobi and other towns, especially the women. The Captain was in his glory, going back with crowds of women and children aboard.

One hazy night I was trying to see the light on an island on the coast to see if the ship was properly on her course. I, however, did not pick it up, so within half an hour I went back to see the 3rd mate who was on duty to ask him if he had picked it up. When I got on the bridge, the Captain was entertaining some of the passengers with gramophone music and there was even some dancing on one side of the bridge and the 3rd mate on the other side, straining his eyes looking for the light. Luckily we both picked it up, exactly where it should be, but I was a bit perturbed at the Captain's discipline.

I am not sure if it was about this time our coal bunkers took fire and we could not reach the seat of the fire and we were afraid the ship might go on fire if we did not get it out. Seeing the danger, I got the 2nd mate to tie a rope around me and tie a wet handkerchief round my mouth. So I went crawling along, carrying a hose with me. Luckily I found the fire and put the nozzle of the hose on it, or rather near it. I got back on deck, nearly suffocated, and took a good glass of whisky, hoping that it would revive me. After about an hour I was able to move and within two hours was back to normal. Meantime the pumps were busy and the bunkers got partly flooded and the fire went out.

After a few voyages up and down the coast, the Captain got word from the London Office through the Superintendent in Durban that he was to go home on leave as he had not had leave for five years. I don't think that worried him overmuch, but orders were orders and he left us and went home as passenger in one of the Aberdeen White Star Liners. I was promoted Master of the *"Salamis"*. In a way I was sorry he left for I knew very well it was against his will that he went on leave.

We carried on in the same old way, as sailors usually say. Civilians going north, troops coming back to Durban. I bought an old car (Ford) for practically nothing in Dar-es-Salaam and took it to Durban for use there and left it with a friend while I was away. Licences were not necessary in those days and I don't remember paying any road taxes; perhaps my friend did for he used it while I was away. Everyone I met and knew on the East African coast was clamouring for a passage to Durban.

Two nurse friends of my cousin Jessie went to see their Colonel to allow them to travel with me and he refused as he had to go by the rota or list, but they said, 'The Captain of the *"Salamis"* will give us berths in his room and he himself will sleep in the chartroom.'

To this he agreed. I had told them this before the interview.

On the way to Durban we called at Port Amelia to pick up a few troops who came down from the bush. The military landing officer there was a very old friend. He was Captain of a ship at the beginning of the war, but got torpedoed and was afterwards M.P. for some Glasgow constituency. Anyway, he had the habit of bouncing into my room without knocking and shouting, 'Hello, Murchie!'

But, alas, on this occasion he was completely flabbergasted on seeing one woman with her legs over the bunk having a cup of tea and another with her nightie on lying on the settee. He rushed out as if he had seen the devil and was wondering if women were now in charge of the ship.

I remember one afternoon sailing for Zanzibar and, as usual with the *"Salamis"*, she took a heavy list while the Chief Engineer was changing fresh water from one tank to another. They were in the bottom of the ship and were the only tanks in the ship. She was built without what is known today as a double bottom. Evidently someone from headquarters was watching the ship after we sailed and noticed that we took a heavy list to starboard. He reported the critical condition, as he thought, and immediately wireless messages were flying out to us, asking if the ship was in a seaworthy condition. I assured them that there was nothing wrong and by the time we had covered the short distance to Zanzibar, the ship was on an even keel.

I made several voyages up and down the East Coast of Africa, carrying white troops to Durban and sometimes Nigerians and Gold Coast troops for transferring into home bound troopships. Early in 1919 we got word that the ship was to be reconditioned in Durban and handed over to the owners. So we had a long spell there while this job was going on - about five or six weeks with nothing much to do but gallivant around the town. During our stay there word came from London that the ship was sold to the Canadian National Company and was chartered to load a cargo from East African ports to Marseilles and then to London to be handed over there. Shortly afterwards the ship *"Gujarat"*, belonging to the Bank Line, arrived at Durban from Calcutta and the Captain said he was not feeling very well and needed leave and, as he was a senior master, the Superintendent should allow him to go home and take charge of the *"Salamis"*. To this the Superintendent agreed, so I was transferred there and then to the *"Gujarat"* and her Captain took over the *"Salamis"*. The change did not bother me at all. In a couple of days I sailed for East London, Port Elizabeth, Mossel Bay and Cape Town, and in due course arrived back in Durban to load for India. While there I was informed that the change of masters caused a lot of annoyance in London, where it was agreed that the Master should be left in the ship till her arrival in London. The Superintendent did not know this and, as a cable took ten days at that time to get a reply owing, presumably, to congestion due to military and naval matters, the Superintendent did not ask permission to exchange masters. The Captain took his wife, Mrs. Clayton, home with him, as she was in South Africa during the whole war.

I heard no more news of the *"Salamis"* until several years afterwards in Basrah, Iraq, where I met a man who had been 2nd mate of her during a gale on her way from Avonmouth to Montreal. I have probably already said that the *"Salamis"* was the worst ship I was ever in for rolling, for she had no bilge keels or, as sailors call them, Rolling Chocks. Evidently, the gale she was in was very severe and she could not make any headway against it, and so went broadside to the heavy sea. Finally, the Donkey Boiler which was situated above the main boiler began to get loose and finally got adrift and began rolling from one side of the ship to the other. The crew thought it would go through the side of the ship, but it did not for it fell into the main engines and broke the main steampipe. The ship became helpless and finally had to be towed. It was sold, probably for scrap. I liked the old ship. During the three years I was mate and master of her, I never slept out of either the mate's or master's bunks, except, occasionally, on the chartroom settee. I missed her when I left her, even though we had many narrow escapes aboard her.

On our last trip from East Africa, the largest number of our troops were men stationed in offices in large and small towns in East Africa and nearly every one of them had a monkey. The officer commanding got very annoyed, and told everyone that the monkeys must be left or put ashore. One large baboon, however, was left on board or rather was a stowaway. A Durban apprentice took charge of it and it was to be delivered in due course to the zoo. While we were coaling ship, the baboon was tied up close to the funnel. The baboon somehow or other got loose and the first thing he did was to throw lumps of coal at the coalmen and they ran away. I immediately ordered apprentice Rennie to take the baboon to the zoo. He, however, only took it to his own house and left it. There his mother and sister got an awful fright when they returned home from their shopping to see a baboon in their back yard.

I was now on the way to India in the *"Gujarat"*, a different kind of ship which carried 25 first class passengers and a large number of deck passengers. The mate left the ship when I joined her so I had to promote the 2nd mate's certificate to mate and the 3rd mate who had not a certificate at all to 2nd mate and an apprentice was promoted to 3rd mate.

Our first port of call after leaving Durban was Colombo and we got there safely, and the young men without certificates appeared to me as able as the ones with certificates, but whether they would be able to take the ship's position, I am unable to say. The shipping master in Durban was not too keen on our sailing without another man with a certificate aboard, but in the end yielded as we could not find a man. After a short stay in Colombo we sailed for Calcutta where a 2nd mate from one of the ships from home was given the job as 1st mate; a young man of 21, very able. I had the old crew of the *"Salamis"* aboard for repatriation to Hong Kong. They were passengers with us, all good and faithful men.

Our Chief Engineer was a taciturn Scot. A very fine man in many ways, but he had set ideas in his mind, and although he hailed from the south of Scotland, he was more superstitious than the Highlanders.

He said to me one day that I should take a good glass of pure whisky every morning when I got out of bed. This rather startled me for I was a strict abstainer.

'But,' said I, 'why do you suggest such a course in a tropical country?'

'Ah,' he said. 'I have been doing it for years and I never got malaria.'

He said it was a grand cure and was just the thing to do in a hot climate and especially so in a town like Calcutta. Indeed it would keep all diseases out of your system, but to get the real benefit it must be taken just as you get out of bed.

'Well, Chief,' I said. 'I have not had malaria and never tasted strong drink.' But I did not convince him.

We loaded up for South Africa and the balance was to be picked up in Colombo. On the way down river with 25 European passengers aboard and a large number of Indians as deck passengers, we had to anchor till the tide came in to take us over the most treacherous bar on the river Hooghly. The pilot was taking no risks so he dropped the anchors and kept a man at the wheel and the 3rd mate on the bridge. What is known as the "Freshets" were very bad with enormous floods coming down. The pilot came down to my cabin for a drink and, while enjoying his dram, we heard the wheel on the bridge moving about a lot and we both rushed on to the bridge to find that the ship had taken a fearful sheer and dragged her anchors. We put the engines full speed ahead and our stern smelt the ground and the rudder post touched the moving, swilling sand in the bar; so although we had 75 fathoms of cable out it snapped and the other anchor could not hold her, so it looked as if we were going to be stranded on the bar. The ship took a very heavy and dangerous list and so I ordered the lifeboats to be lowered to the level of the rail. The Indian passengers I am afraid got worried and were moving towards the lifeboats and one European got frantic. He had been shell shocked during the war. However, I persuaded the passengers to remain calm and as the list was not increasing there was no danger. Within a few minutes, and all of a sudden, the ship became upright and we all realised that the "bore" or the tide had turned in and lifted the ship off the sandbank. So it was heave up our one anchor and sail outwards. The pilot did not leave the bridge and kept the engines going full speed ahead. He said by keeping the engines full ahead the propellers were swilling away the sand and that it therefore did not collect around the ship and embed her. Shifting sands are very dangerous at all times and one or two ships were lost on the bank we touched and, if my memory serves me right, with heavy loss of lives at least in one ship.

We moved down river and in no time were dropping the pilot by midnight. That was my worst experience on shifting sands and it did look frightening when our cable parted.

No sooner had the pilot gone away than the Chief Engineer came up to my room to tell me that some of the engineers had bought peacock feathers in Calcutta and he said very gravely how unlucky they were aboard ship and how near we were to disaster just the night before. We were bound to meet with further ill luck unless all the peacock feather were dumped into the sea. Already, he said, he had got the 2nd and 3rd engineers to chuck theirs into the sea, but the Chief Officer had some and I should give him a severe talking to and get him to throw his into the Bay of Bengal.

'Well, Chief,' I said, 'I never heard before that peacock feathers were unlucky.'

If I told the Chief Officer to get rid of them he would think that I was interfering with his private affairs and take me to be an old superstitious ass and, really, I could not myself believe that peacock feathers could in any way govern our future voyages.

The Chief fully believed they would interfere with our future voyages and he said, 'Just you wait and you will see that I am right.'

I told the Chief Officer on the quiet what the Chief was telling me and we both laughed at the idea.

In a few days we got into Colombo, Ceylon, to load further cargo for South Africa and while in harbour the Chief Officer got busy moving the spare anchor which was lying on the foremain deck on to the starboard bow to replace the anchor we had lost on the bar in the Hooghly. While he was doing so the anchor some way or other moved in the slings and slightly damaged the cockwheels on one of the deck winches. This was reported to the Chief Engineer and he was, of course, extremely annoyed and accused the Chief Officer of being careless, his carelessness being due to the fact that he had peacock feathers in his room and was therefore harbouring evil spirits in the ship.

We got to South Africa without further annoyance, but in arriving back from Cape Town and anchoring off the Durban breakwater we nearly lost another anchor. The pilot came aboard rather late and it was getting dark, but nevertheless he decided to take us in and put the ship under the coal shoots. Just then it came on to blow and it looked as if the pilot could not manage to berth the ship, and on several occasions it looked as if the ship would drift on to other ships, or that we would have to go out to sea again. After struggling with the wind and the darkness for three hours we at last got into the berth. The Chief Engineer was winning his point and pointed out the waste of steam and coal in trying to get the ship berthed and the cost to the owners just because someone was foolish enough to believe that peacock feathers were harmless at sea.

All went well in Durban and we loaded the ship with cargo which was mostly bark for tanning for Madras. We were less than six hours at sea when a big heavy Zulu came up on deck from the hold and looked round to find that he could not see anything but the boundless ocean. He was sent up to me but nobody in the ship could understand his language, but we gathered that he had fallen asleep down the hold when loading the cargo. So we discharged him in Colombo and he was sent back in one of the other vessels bound for South Africa.

In due course we got to Madras and were tied to a buoy in the harbour with our own cable. Our anchor was hanging by a wire from the bow. The cargo was discharged and we were due to sail at midnight, so I suggested to the Chief Officer to put slip ropes round the buoy and get the cable attached to our own anchor before it got dark. This he did, but to make it easier for himself and easier to shackle the cable to the anchor, he thought he would lower the anchor by slacking the wire round the bollard, although I told him not to do this what ever happened. But young men think they know better, so immediately he began to lower the anchor which was several tons in weight. The wire carried away and, of course, the anchor dropped to the bottom of the harbour. I never said anything to him when he told me the story, but got into a boat and ran up to the harbour master's office to get a diver. The office was closed, but someone knew where the diver lived. Into a taxi I jumped, got the diver and within an hour the anchor was secured to the cable and the diver was all smiles when I gave him 30/-. We sailed at midnight.

Next morning at 7am I walked on to the bridge to have a yarn with the Chief Officer who was on watch. The first words he said to me were that he had thrown all his peacock feathers overboard. I laughed. We arrived safely in Calcutta the next day.

With all the peacock feathers overboard, life on board became normal and we loaded in Calcutta for South Africa with the usual general cargo. In Durban we had to take on board a big heavy launch for a very wealthy Cape Town business man. This launch was as long as the foredeck and it came alongside in the evening with a man to see that it was safely placed on board. The evening turned out to be very nasty with a strong or moderate gale from the south and heavy showers. Our Superintendent had to go home as he was suffering from a heavy cold and influenza, and told me to keep my eye on the people in the shed and see that all the cargo booked went on board. I thought I would have a look around in the shed, but meantime the launch arrived alongside, so I told the Chief Officer to leave the launch till the weather moderated, even till the morning if necessary. However, while I was in the shed the Chief Officer thought the wind and sea were going down and it would save him a lot of trouble if he got the launch aboard. He put the slings on it but omitted to put spreaders (that is, pieces of wood across each slings level with the gunwale) to prevent undue strain on the hull where the slings go round. Anyway, when I got aboard there was the launch almost aboard and the youngster who was sent from his office to see the launch safely aboard on the saloon deck looking on. When it was nicely placed above the deck of the ship and was ready for lowering, the young man said to me that he could now go back to his office and truthfully say that he had seen the launch aboard the ship. I replied, yes, but while he was turning his back to go, the launch then being only one foot above the deck, the slings suddenly went through the hull.

I noticed what happened and so did the Chief Officer, but nobody else, so I shouted, 'Cover the launch up at once and lash her well to the deck.'

This was done and we sailed at 6am the next day as per our schedule with good weather. When we got outside there was a heavy sea on due to the gale of the day before, but on the whole the ship wasn't making heavy weather of it. The launch, I presume, was insured, but I was not sure if it was insured if we damaged it.

Officers and Captains of ships in my young days were trained that their first duty was to be loyal to the owners. In any Bill of Lading, acts of God, perils of the deep and restraint of Princes, etc, were the prominent items. I therefore suggested to the Chief Officer that he put in his logbook that heavy seas coming aboard moved the launch but that the lashings held, so that was the cause of the broken timber on the sides of the launch. Lloyds' agents were very sympathetic on our arrival in Cape Town and were thankful that the launch wasn't washed overboard. Repairs would not cost much and the insurance would pay. When I was saying goodbye to the Chief Officer when the ship was sold, we were going over all our voyages together. He then mentioned to me that he got £10 from somebody in Cape Town for his seamanship and attention for managing to bring the launch into Cape Town with only minor damage. I could only laugh at the whole thing and said that he needed the £10 as he was continually hard up.

On calling at Durban on our way back to India, two of the sisters from a charitable R.C. hospital came aboard to gather money. In fact they came aboard every voyage and I knew them very well. They called on all the officers and engineers and I saw them coming up the ladder into the saloon deck.

The Chief Officer was talking to me at the time in front of my room and, of course, saw them through the corner of his eye and said to me, 'Good heavens. Here are the sisters of mercy coming up and I have not a halfpenny in the world.'

I said, 'Jump behind my door.'

And no sooner said than done; I was chatting with them and gave them my usual contribution. Then they remarked that they could not find the Chief Officer anywhere. I said that he was in my room so one of them walked in and there, stupidly, was the Chief behind my door.

We all laughed and he said to me, 'Please give them something from me,' which I did.

Immediately they left he swore and told me he would never pay me back the money I had given away for him, and I don't remember that he ever did, but we were 'as pally as ever' and he saw the joke.

One of the sisters was a very attractive young woman and on one occasion she went aboard a ship to try and get money for the deserving hospital or orphanage. There was a gallant young Irishman as master of this ship and when she approached him, he said, 'If you will give me a kiss, I will try to do my best to extract all the money I can from the officers and crew.'

She appeared horrified and naturally refused, but in spite of all her arguments that it would be very unseemly, he would not give in.

She was just on the point of going away, when she turned round and said, 'For God's sake I will give you a kiss,' to which he replied, 'And for God's sake hurry up about it.'

She got as promised a good bit of money for the orphanage. These sisters did a lot of good work and many a soul was thankful for their kindness, love and hospitality.

About this time we had a weekend in Durban, which was unusual, for we always tried to be at sea for weekends and I was as anxious as anyone to get the ship out of port on Saturday nights, very much to the annoyance of the officers and crew. I was imbued with one idea only and that was to be always on the 'go'; hurry into port, hurry out of port; and I chased people around to this end. This weekend I mentioned above, a friend came aboard and told me that he was taking some friends over to the island in a launch and would I come? I was never fond of picnics for it meant having your food out of all sorts of dishes and sitting on grass with flies and insects buzzing around. I always prefer my food at a table and in comfort. However, I agreed and said that the Chief Officer was very fond of picnics. So when it was mentioned to him, he was all agog. Several girls were in the party and I soon noticed that the Chief Officer was edging nearer and nearer to the best looking girl there. He saw her again the following voyage, and when our ship was sold he joined one of the other ships on the run and at one time I really thought he had married her, till during the last war I was travelling home by plane from Basrah to Durban, then by ship from there home and, of course, met my old friends in Durban. The mate was now managing director of a large stevedoring firm.

I naturally said to his wife, 'We met before in 1919.'

She said, 'No, that was my sister you met then.'

We went straight from Durban to Moulmein in Burma to load large logs of teak for South Africa for the return journey. While in port the first plane to travel direct from Great Britain passed over and it caused great excitement in this small town. The labourers on board loading the teakwood gave up work and gazed at the sky and all the men down the holds rushed up on deck to see (as they called it) the biggest bird they had ever seen. Nothing else was talked about for hours.

We were not long out of Moulmein on our way to Calcutta when the weather began to be a bit peculiar, which was unusual in the Bay of Bengal and I knew a cyclone was in the making. I was very anxious to get to the pilot boat before dark. When, however, midday came the sun was right overhead and at times obscured so I got a poor fix for the latitude and, knowing very well that cyclones cause unknown currents, I was afraid my position was at least incorrect. Luckily at 3pm, I put the supposed altitude of the planet Venus on my sextant and suddenly about 3.30pm, when a scudding cloud left a blue patch in the sky, there it was, not far from the horizon. I got the correct latitude of Venus and a correct longitude from the sun. My position was 10 miles out, so I altered course straight for the pilot boat and got the pilot aboard at 5.30pm, and she followed us into the shelter of Sangor Island as the cyclone was approaching fast.

When we got into the anchorage we dropped the two anchors and kept the engines going slowly ahead while the cyclone was at its worst. When the worst of it was over we proceeded up the river to Calcutta. I was thankful we got the pilot, for Bengal cyclones can be very severe and often cause damage to the best found ships.

Our stay in Calcutta, taking aboard the usual cargo, did not take long and our call in Colombo for cargo was usually of short duration. When I was on my first voyage on this run, the Superintendent in Durban complained to me of the heavy breakages in the tea chests, so I was always on the alert to stop it. Most of the breakages were caused by the stevedoring labour throwing the cases about, so I stopped it, with the result that our claims for damage were practically nil.

I had often heard that Australians were the greatest tea drinkers in the world with the South Africans next, which I came to believe was the truth, judging by all the tea we took aboard, voyage after voyage.

We did the usual round to Cape Town and back to Durban where we heard that the ship was sold with delivery in Calcutta early in the New Year, 1920. This was sad news for we were very happy in the old ship. We were to load a cargo of coal in Durban for Colombo. We had never carried coal before so we had a longer stay there than usual. I had friends in Durban who were anxious to go and see a great friend of theirs called MacNaughton who had a farm about 100 miles up country. The old farmer MacNaughton was one of the old school. He told me great stories about the times he used to carry goods with horses and oxen to Johannesburg, when Johannesburg was a village of a few corrugated iron stores and houses. The visit was arranged to be on a Sunday and we went in a six seater car. I asked the Chief Officer, Mr. Chicken, to come along with us.

Lunch was ready when we arrived and a big crowd of us were at the table with the worthy MacNaughton at the head carving the chickens.

All of a sudden when he came to serve the Chief Officer, Mr. Chicken, he said, 'Mr. Chocolate, will you have some chicken?'

After lunch Mr. MacNaughton took the Chief Officer and me to see his prize Friesian cattle and asked me to take a photo of them with my camera. So I went down to a knoll with the Chief Officer following me. I took my stance up on this mound to get a good photo as the cattle marched by below me. Just then the big bull started scraping the ground and roaring, but as a boy I was used to Highland Cattle so took no notice but proceeded to get my photos which, by the way, turned out to be very good. All this time I thought the Chief Officer was behind me, but when he heard the bull roaring he took to his heels and was out of breath by the time he reached MacNaughton at the stables. I walked back just in time to hear the old farmer slating sailors for being such cowards with ordinary quiet cattle.

On the voyage back we had a full complement of 1st class passengers to Colombo and also a large number of deck passengers. Just as we finished loading our cargo of coal I was walking along to the ship from the office and saw an oldish man and his wife and a young woman at the bottom of the gangway. When I got up to them they asked me if I knew if the Captain was aboard as they had a letter for him. I said I was the Captain, so the young lady laughed.

I asked why she was laughing and she said, 'Because I thought that all captains of ships were oldish men with beards.'

I suppose I looked younger than 35. They gave me the letter from the agents up country with the information that the young lady was bound for Ceylon where she was to marry a planter and I was to look after her. Then later on the deck passengers came aboard with all sorts of luggage including beds and chairs. We were due to sail at noon, but, at about 11.45am, C.I.D. men from Pretoria came on board and told me that they were extremely sorry but they would have to delay the sailing of the ship as they heard that smuggled gold was aboard. Gold was prohibited to go out of South Africa. The pilot came on board and he and I were on the bridge watching the searchers working hard amongst the luggage of the Indian deck passengers. They did not seem to make much progress and I suppose they were getting fed up, but there was a big burly chap amongst them who was wielding an axe and he came down with full force on the big wooden arm of a very long chair and what came pouring out of the arm but dozens of sovereigns! It was a big haul. As nobody would admit to ownership of the chair or the sovereigns, they took them all ashore and we were allowed to proceed on our voyage. Little did I know that this was to be my last look at Durban for more than 20 years, for my next trip there was by flying boat on the 27th December 1940 on my way home on leave from Basrah, Iraq.

We weren't long in discharging in Colombo, so sailed for Calcutta to hand the ship over to the new owners from Hong Kong. Strange to say we all worked hard to get the ship in a spick and span condition and on our arrival in Calcutta the Superintendent was amazed how clean the ship was after discharging coal. The new owners were quite happy at the old ship's condition, so they took her over with the minimum of fuss and trouble. All the officers and engineers were transferred to some of the other ships which were either in Calcutta, or due there soon. The Chief Officer was made Chief Officer of the *"Kathiwar"* which was plying on the same run, that is Burma, Calcutta to South Africa and East African ports via Colombo. I was in a hotel in Calcutta for two weeks before I got a passage home. Every ship was full up and there was great difficulty in getting passages owing to the rush of people wanting home after the war. Eventually I got a passage in the S.S. *"Botanist"*, a cargo boat, so I was glad to be getting home after being away for over four years.

When we were approaching Ceylon before breakfast (the east coast part of it), I was very surprised to see the ship so close to the land, for in all my voyages there I never got close to the land in those parts, and although I was a passenger I thought we were far too near the land. About 11am, we struck a reef which is known as the Horseshoe Reef. The ship got off but in trying to get out we grounded again and there the ship stuck and began to sink and by the afternoon or evening the after part of the ship was awash, and the other nine passengers, all men, were deeply concerned so they asked me if they should go to sleep. I said that I thought the ship was on the bottom and would not move an inch and in any case I was going to sleep. Actually, we all slept (at least I did, very soundly) on the bridge deck as the weather was very hot. Next day the ship S.S. *"Martaban"* came to our assistance and anchored outside the reef. So the crew got the lifeboats out and started to ferry ourselves and our luggage to the S.S. *"Martaban"*. The crew were Indians with four English quartermasters. I volunteered to help them in the boats, so I went in the first boat with the passengers. We had great difficulty in getting a very lame man (both his legs were bad) into the boat and he could not possibly walk up the gangway of the *"Martaban"*, although there was very little sea or movement of the ship. I shouted up to the Chief Officer of the *"Martaban"* to send a large coal basket down if he had any. In a few minutes the basket was lowered; it was quite a haul up as the ship was light, but nevertheless Mr. Murray was quite comfortable in the basket when hauled up by the winch. The other passengers all got aboard safely and I went back for the luggage to the wrecked ship.

I took an oar both going and coming and the quartermaster said to the mate on our return, 'I don't know who that passenger is but, by God, he knows how to row and handle an oar!'

Seeing I was used to rowing boats in my native village from a very early age, I never lost the art. By the time we got the luggage in the *"Martaban"* the salvage vessel with all their gear and stevedores were aboard the *"Botanist"*. Nothing much was salvaged so the ship was a total wreck. We were made comfortable on the *"Martaban"* and the Captain told me to go into his cabin for the night, as he was going to sleep in the chartroom, as he would have to be most of the night on the bridge while they were rounding the southern points of Ceylon. We were landed the next day in Colombo and all the passengers had their own friends and I presume stayed with them. I was put into the Galleface Hotel, one of the most luxurious out east and there I remained for a fortnight and never in my life did I have such an easy life. I got up in the morning fairly early, went into the hotel bathing pool and then breakfast. Later on I took a run into town and then back for lunch and to read. I never thought it was possible to have such an easy time.

The night I was aboard the *"Martaban"* and sleeping very comfortably in the Captain's cabin, the quartermaster opened the door of the cabin and shouted, 'Point de Galle lighthouse abeam, sir.'

I so often heard the same shout when in my own ship that for the moment I did not realize I was a passenger. When, however, I opened my eyes and looked at my surroundings I remembered the Captain was in the chartroom, so I shouted, 'Go to hell, I am not master of this ship.'

And I went on the other 'tack' and went sound asleep again. It was such a feeling of relief.

I heard of one Captain who, when he retired, took the senior quartermaster who had sailed with him most of his life ashore with him and gave him a room in the house for himself. His duties were to call the Captain very early so that he could say to him, 'Go to hell', and then go to sleep till his breakfast was ready.

After a fortnight in the hotel I got word to join the *"Explorer"*, a sister of the *"Botanist"* and all went well on the passage home and we arrived in London on a very cold day, so I took a taxi to the office and I felt so cold that I stopped the taxi while on the way and bought a heavy overcoat. Being so long out east and voyaging for four years, mostly in the tropics, it was natural that I should feel cold.

After a few days in London and settling my account, I thought I would go straight home. I called on my cousin, Margaret Murchison, who was a nurse in a private hospital in London. I decided to go by Glasgow where my brothers Murdo and Kenneth were - one in the University and the other learning engineering - and not due home on leave for over a month.

I spent a couple of days in Glasgow. My brother Murdo told me a funny story about my brother John. John was in Glasgow for a week staying with Murdo in the same lodgings. The landlady was concerned about Murdo not eating enough, but what she did not know was that Murdo had a nice big lunch when studying at the university and therefore had light breakfasts and high teas. When John arrived he ate everything that Murdo left for he had always a hearty appetite. The kindly old lady was so pleased that Murdo was eating his food better since his brother arrived, and she naturally put it down to the fact that Murdo was so fond of John and pined for him so much when he was not with him that he went off his food. There was quite a brotherly feeling between them but not to the extent that the old woman imagined.

I left Glasgow to go and stay with Aunt Jessie who had a sheep farm at Coulin near Kinlochewe. She had been advised to give it up when her husband died seven years earlier, but she was an extremely determined woman (and over 70) and so ignored everybody. But now that the boom in sheep and wool was coming to a close, I thought I would influence her and give her advice. I laid the law down when I got there in the evening and pointed out to her that prices would fall within the next few years. She did not keep it for more than a few years more, but, looking back on it, it would have been better to let her toil away, as she was at a loose end till she died in 1926.

From there I went home. My cousin, Nan MacDonald, was telling me that my mother was wondering why I did not write home from London, for Maggie Murchison wrote home to say I called. My father was listening to the conversation and when Nan said that William would be too busy to write letter, calling here and there and in the office, etc, my father said our William could write all we wanted to know with his big toe if he was busy with his hands. Actually, I was very diligent at writing home all the years I had been at sea, but on this occasion I really thought I would be home myself sooner than a letter would reach them.

When I packed my sailor's bag in Calcutta, I never thought it would be the last time. As I was away for over four years and, as I said already, never slept out of a ship's bunk till I left the *"Gujarat"*, it was time I had a holiday. I enjoyed being at home and was happy to wander around the villages of Applecross for almost three months.

One day I got a letter from London to say that I was to go there the following week so that arrangements could be made about my future employment. When I got there, to my surprise, I was told that I was to proceed to Basrah, Iraq, to superintend several tugs and barges which the firm had purchased to run a cargo service on the River Tigris from Basrah to Baghdad. This was a completely new job: one which I was not sure that I had the ability to do properly. However, I had in those day sufficient confidence to tackle anything, so I stayed in the office, looking over all the details I could find regarding the new job I had taken on. It was indeed very difficult to find out much and the correspondence from the office was not very comforting, for as far as I could make out, the tugs were continually breaking down and the boilers were giving continual trouble.

My passage was booked for the end of August 1920 sailing from Glasgow. The office was closed for the bank holidays in August so I went to Edinburgh and met Proby MacRae and there we got engaged. We both travelled to London and had a nice time there. Time was getting on and I was to go home to Applecross to get on with my packing. We both travelled north, so I had about a week in Applecross and Loch Carron and just left in time to get aboard the ship (an old cargo boat) that was taking me to Basrah.

I spent 20 years at sea altogether on all sorts of ships. It was a hard life, especially in the sailing ships and even the tramps I was in before the mast were not much better, except that we got fresher food. On the other hand, a sailing ship going along at a good speed in a steady wind gave one a great lift and compensated one for the bad weather and the bad food.